FOREWORD BY
DAVID POPOVICI

FASTING

REDISCOVERING THE
ANCIENT PATHWAYS

MICHAEL DOW

Copyright © 2016 by Michael Dow

Fasting

by Michael Dow

Printed in the United States of America

ISBN 978-0-9892185-2-8

All rights reserved. No part of this document may be reproduced or transmitted in any form, by any means (electronic, photocopying, recording, or otherwise) without the written permission of the author.

Unless otherwise indicated, Scripture quotations are taken from the New American Standard Bible®. Copyright © 1960, 1962, 1963, 1968, 1971, 1972, 1973, 1975, 1977, 1995 by The Lockman Foundation. Used by permission. (www.Lockman.org)

Scripture quotations marked "NIV" are taken from the Holy Bible, New International Version®, NIV®. Copyright © 1973, 1978, 1984, 2011 by Biblica, Inc.® Used by permission. All rights reserved worldwide.

Scripture quotations marked "ESV" are taken the Holy Bible, English Standard Version. Copyright © 2001 by Crossway Bibles, a publishing ministry of Good News Publishers.

Scripture quotations marked (HCSB) are taken the Holman Christian Standard Bible. Copyright © 1999, 2000, 2002, 2003, 2009 by Holman Bible Publishers, Nashville Tennessee. All rights reserved.

Scripture quotations marked "KJV" are taken from the King James Version of the Bible. Public domain.

Scripture quotations marked "NLT" are taken from the Holy Bible, New Living Translation. Copyright © 1996, 2004, 2007, 2013 by Tyndale House Foundation. Used by permission of Tyndale House Publishers Inc., Carol Stream, Illinois 60188. All rights reserved.

All definitions are taken from www.merriam-webster.com.

Dedication

I dedicate this book to those who are hungry for more of God. This is dedicated to those, who like Enoch, have chosen not to live under the lie that there isn't any more of God to be had or experienced. I dedicate this to those whose sole desire is to walk with Him who is life and to be taken up, even as Enoch, into that life in its fullness. I dedicate this book to every passionate traveler of the ancient pathways of union with Christ that has tasted and has seen that He is good and now is relentlessly after the One that has bid us to come to Himself.

I dedicate this book to a breed of follower that Jesus is awakening in these last days that will forsake all things, at any cost, in order to be found within the divine embrace.

As the travelers of old would say when they disembarked from the coast of America heading to preach Christ in distant lands among a people that had not heard, let our hearts' cry be such as theirs, "May the Lamb that was slain receive the reward of His suffering!"

May this cry recalibrate our hearts and set our lives upon a path that will settle for nothing less than living constantly before the face of the one true King, Jesus Christ!

Table of Contents

Acknowledgments vii
Foreword ix
Introduction xv

1   Explanation 25
2   Fascination 39
3   Objections 47
4   Self 55
5   Habit 65
6   Unbelief 81
7   Deliverance 97
8   Types 117
9   Practical 139
10   Expectations 153
11   Purifying 167

About the Author 183
About the Ministry 185

Acknowledgments

To my wife, Anna, and three beautiful children, Ariyah, Josiah, and Emma, I thank you. Outside of Christ you are the greatest joys this life has given to me. I thank you for believing in me and continually encouraging me day by day to press into Him who is life.

Thank you to David Popovici for writing the foreword for this project. Your life is a testimony to what is available if a man will hand himself over to God. Thank you for provoking those close to you with your life itself.

Thank you to John Garrett for your help in preparing this project. You are a brother that I hold near and dear to my heart.

Thank you to Kathy Curtis for your work and excellence in editing and typesetting. It is a continued joy to work with you and to be a beneficiary of your efforts.

Thank you to Blake Vasek for designing such an extraordinary cover for this project and visually capturing the heart of it all.

Thank you to those who have walked with me closely in this life and have been a continued strength as I have sought to give more of myself to Christ. Thank you to everyone who has ever encouraged me to "keep going," or to "not give up." Your words have continued to ring loud in my heart as I have relentlessly chosen to not let go of the person of Christ.

Foreword

Fasting is not an end, but a means and an expression of a longing to be filled with God. Let's take a look at why. There is a God in the heavens whose desire is to reveal Himself to His creation; to be made known, even more, to walk in intimate union and rule in the midst of them. Yet He does so in accordance to His own nature and terms.

He does so by and through the realm of the Spirit. The tragedy of the fall from glory is that mankind was kicked out of the garden, which was the overlapping of two realms: glorified spirit life existing on the earth. Mankind internally died, was separated from the *LIFE* of the Spirit and cast into the realm of fallen nature where the five senses of the natural man and appetites rule supreme.

Jesus' arrival as a man on the earth was the beginning of the Kingdom come. One that will be wrapped up in His return, when He forever unites the heavens and the earth. His life in the body was both a living expression and mediation to enable humanity to once again live by the *LIFE* of the Spirit. But man had lost his way and Jesus became the way.

Because of sin, man was cast into a downward spiral of twisted sinful desires and dead religion. Man had ultimately lost sight of the *Divine Face*. The Scriptures testify that the Man Jesus is the ultimate expression of God.[1] Throughout His life in the body, Jesus lived as the revelation of the Divine through two main channels: the revelation of the *cross* and the life of the *Spirit*.

The cross was not only an event to be accomplished, but also the expression of His internal nature. He laid down His life, as a way of life, and He was made alive, as a way of life, through loving union with His Father. For the first time since the garden humanity watched the overlap of two realms in full display, perfectly alive in a man.

The cross represents death. Jesus says, "If anyone wishes to come after Me, he must deny himself, take up his cross and follow Me."[2] Jesus said, *"If any man wishes…,"* because being joined to Him who is *LIFE*, starts in our desires.

---

[1] Heb. 1:3
[2] Matt. 16:24

Foreword

It is because God in His goodness has chosen to reveal Himself in and to us that we even want Him. We have seen something, touched something, heard something, not of this world, something that satisfies beyond the layers of this natural life. So what will we do now?

You, my friend, are invited to follow, to live in His presence; to participate with Him in the holy beauty of His eternal purposes. Jesus said if this is your desire, *if any man wishes*, you must deny and voluntarily choose to bear the cross that you may be equipped and able to live in that realm. The realm of His *LIFE,* presence, and joint participation.

It is not that God will reject you if you do not deny and carry your cross. But by rejecting Christ you are by default rejecting Him. The measure to which we choose to embrace the cross determines how well we will host His *LIFE* within us. The gravitation of the world and the natural man pull away from the Lord of life, but the cross beautifully condemns us to *LIFE*. In the Kingdom gravity pulls upward. Upward is resurrection, and resurrection only happens after death, by crucifying our bodily desires. Fasting puts us into the stream of the Spirit's upward pull.

As people we often measure ourselves in terms of our doing more than our being, our activities more than our identity. Many people have said things like,

"I'm not one of those fasting guys," or, "Fasting is not my calling, not my gifting." That is not the best way to approach fasting.

The heart of someone stepping into fasting should be, "I have a desire birthed by God within me to follow Him, to be with Him, to live in Him and Him in me." If this is your heart, well then, fasting is for you. Jesus prescribed the expression of righteous living on the earth when He spoke of heaven's economy on the holy mountain. Righteous living is the life of the age to come exemplified in the present.

In Matthew chapters 5 through 7, Jesus' message was first a self-depiction of His person and His way of life in the Spirit, and then an open invitation to all to live in the realm of His loving rule. Fasting was not man's idea. Even if it might be misrepresented, it's still valid according to Jesus.

Everything under the sun has been misrepresented on some level, but that never means we ought to reject what is authentic. Fasting is an expression of holy desire. Fasting is the offering up of our appetites and natural senses to Him who perfectly fills all that He might open them up and purify them so that we can house and become a living conduit of His Spirit and Kingdom.

Fasting was instituted by God. It became the field in which the saints were forged, kingdoms were established while others crumbled, when pure hearts mingled fasting with their prayers and devotion to God. Principalities in the heavens were pushed back and archangels were dispatched with divine words from the throne of God when God's people fasted with prayer. Much of history was shaped and influenced by the nameless dozens of believers who gave themselves to lives of fasting; men and women who chose to voluntarily give themselves to the union of the cross and display of the Spirit.

Do you want to taste the kind of brokenness that creates space for deeper measures of God's voice and presence in your life? If so, I encourage you to humble your soul with fasting. Do you desire to grow in purity and sensitivity of heart and spirit? Then turn over your plate today and feast upon the One who is Living Bread.

Heaven's ladder will always rest over a Jacob people; the type of people who will not sell the endless inheritance according to His riches in glory like Esau did. This is the generation like Jacob who seek the face of God.[3] Those who will be a John the Baptist kind of people, who live set apart and behold the Lamb. A people like John who had the love, humility, and courage of God worked within him, in his own

---

[3] Ps. 24:6

generation, to stand for truth in the face of rulers, yet fade into the shadows in the presence of Jesus. A man well equipped to joyfully offer to God his head during the time of testing because he was first conditioned by the consistent offering up of his stomach.

Precious saint, today heaven grants you the privileged invitation to give God your life. Give Him your body. Give Him your appetites. Open your heart wide and He will fill it. Man shall not live on bread alone; fast and pray.[4]

David Popovici
Founder of Kingdom Gospel Mission

---

[4] Matt. 4:4

Introduction

I am thankful for the opportunity to share this with you right now, right here in this moment of your life and the age that is unfolding around us. I am thankful for the privilege to implore you with all that I am to no longer live this life for yourself, but rather to surrender all of that which you desire to be most into the hands of Jesus. I am thankful that God has allowed our paths to cross in the form of this book. These pages, I believe, can help bring you into an encounter with Jesus as you continue on pursuing His face.

There is an ancient pathway that many have found yet few have chosen to travel. There is a rugged road that requires a great price that many are not willing to pay. There is an invitation set before all men who have come to believe in Jesus Christ, the Son of God. It is an invitation to continue on with Him in a place of deep intimacy and communion that some have willingly chosen to forfeit.

I would like to invite you to find Him at the end of this pathway. As an ambassador for Christ and His Kingdom I intend to provoke you to make a move in this direction. As one who has seen Him, been with Him, and faithfully followed Him down these narrow paths, I am honored to relay a message: He is waiting for you. He is calling you, by name, to come to Him. Today, do not harden your heart if you hear His voice.

> **There are no shortcuts in the Kingdom of God.**

If you have come across this book thinking that found within its pages are shortcuts, gimmicks, or some sort of easy process to get something from God, I hate to be the one to disappoint. But before we even have an opportunity to waste more time getting acquainted, this is not one of those books. There are too many of those books that frequent shelves in bookstores. There is a plethora of quick breakthrough, easy-blessing books out there for you. There are no shortcuts in the Kingdom of God.

We live in a day where many stand upon positional truths and use them to excuse their hunger for God and anything more. We are in a time where people exempt their pursuit of God with certain doctrinal beliefs stating that we already possess all there is to have in Christ. I know that when we came into this glorious salvation in Christ that we received all of God. My question for you is not if you believe that you have the fullness of God in your life. My question for you is, how much of that fullness are you experiencing on a daily basis? It saddens me to find that most who claim to love Jesus and to walk with Him simply just do not experience Him.

There is an endless well of great experience that awaits the hungry. There is a place of experience far greater than anything you've ever known. There is a living Christ, a Man that is alive from the dead, who beckons to hearts that burn for Him, "Here is the ancient pathway...walk this way... come running this way and find Me here!"

> **There is an endless well of great experience that awaits the hungry.**

All that I've shared within the pages that follow has not come as a result of accumulating information. The things shared in the pages ahead of you have come by revelation and experience. Revelation that the Holy Spirit has installed into my life as I have experienced walking the ancient pathways of fasting. The Holy Spirit has led me into hundreds of days of fasting in my pursuit of Jesus, and on this road I am becoming more like Him.

I don't attempt to boast in these matters or to somehow attempt to build my résumé in your eyes or mind. I share these details so that you can simply have a better understanding that I did not sit with someone who knows about fasting to draw material for this book. I did not read a lot of books on fasting in preparation for this. I have walked with Jesus this way, and He has revealed to me what I know to be much in this area. These are treasures to me, and so my desire is to open up the treasure box to you.

Fasting thins the veil of awareness to the person and presence of Jesus in our lives.

Fasting thins the veil of awareness to the person and presence of Jesus in our lives. Fasting thins the veil of awareness by distancing us from our own carnal desires and needs. Fasting destroys the distractions that so frequently cause us as a people to simply be unaware of Jesus on a day-to-day basis. Fasting awakens our spiritual awareness and causes us to realize the sweet presence of Jesus that has been promised to remain with us to the uttermost parts of the earth and the end of the age.

Awareness, or the state of being aware, is defined as having a present consciousness of someone or something. Awakening spiritual awareness is a game changer. It is the difference between security and insecurity.

Introduction

The book of 2 Kings chapter 6 gives us a situation that I believe beautifully illustrates the difference that awareness can make in your life. The king of Aram is warring against the king of Israel. During the battle the king of Aram finds out that Elisha, the prophet, has been aiding the king of Israel. The king of Aram decides to send his men by night to find Elisha.

Picking up the story in verse 14, "He sent horses and chariots and a great army there, and they came by night and surrounded the city. Now when the attendant of the man of God had risen early and gone out, behold, an army with horses and chariots was circling the city. And his servant said to him, 'Alas, my master! What shall we do?'"[5] Things are not looking good for Elisha and his servant. They are clearly at a disadvantage with what seems to be unfolding right in front of them. After taking inventory of their situation, I don't think there's necessarily anything wrong with the concern of the servant in trying to figure out how they are planning to get out of the mess that they woke up to. These two guys have now found themselves in a situation that is having a great impact upon the heart and life of Elisha's servant; the servant is only aware of what it is that is visible before him.

---

[5] 2 Kings 6:14-15

Verses 15 and 16 give us the picture that we need in order to see the amazing difference that awareness can make in our lives. Elisha's response to his servant is one that is not stated merely according to the facts in the moment. Elisha's response is saturated with awareness, an awareness that will soon change the life of his servant.

"So he answered, 'Do not fear, for those who are with us are more than those who are with them.' Then Elisha prayed and said, 'O Lord, I pray, open his eyes that he may see.' And the Lord opened the servant's eyes and he saw; and behold, the mountain was full of horses and chariots of fire all around Elisha."[6]

This is great! Here you have two men that are standing in the same geographical location, facing the exact same hard evidence in front of them, and yet, they provide us with two completely different reactions. Why? Awareness, that is why. One man, Elisha, stands in a powerful awareness of things unseen, and in fact, prays for the man who is unable to see to have his eyes opened. While Elisha was able to see, his servant was totally unaware until the moment Elisha prayed. Awareness is what makes all the difference in the world.

---

[6] 2 Kings 6:16-17

Introduction

I am not telling you that by eating a cheeseburger Jesus is going to change His proximity to you. It would be foolish to think that because you had a few slices of pizza Jesus would distance Himself. Nothing of the sort is what is being stated here. But we are talking about fasting, and what I am saying is that your awareness of Jesus will be radically affected by the practices of your life. Again, fasting thins the veil of awareness to the presence and person of Jesus. Fasting eliminates the distractions that so commonly cause you to be unaware. Fasting initiates a dismissal of the manipulative efforts of the enemy that cause you to be unconscious to the things unseen.

Your awareness of Jesus will be radically affected by the practices of your life.

In fasting you are empowered. This empowerment is to be free from the vice grip which dominates your thinking and seeing to only be influenced by those things tangibly before you. Fasting breaks you into a place of more than just knowledge of things unseen, but immediate and powerful awareness of things unseen. Fasting initiates an overwhelming consciousness, or awareness, of the nearness of the Lord. It is not just a head knowledge of His nearness that we need. It is the corresponding and always available experiential awareness of that nearness that is needed.

How drastically would your life change if you were more aware of the reality that Jesus is with you? In what ways would you approach your day to day differently if you had an intense awareness to the presence and person of Jesus that was as real to you as the very air you breathe? Like Elisha and his servant, one man was able to react, or act, towards the situations of his life a little differently because of the awareness that he lived in.

It would revolutionize your life if you were more aware of Jesus.

Your current quality of life does not have to be dictated by the things that are tangibly visible before you. Like Elisha's servant, most of us are continually tossed to and fro by the waves of circumstances. Elisha, a man with acute spiritual awareness, was not moved by what he saw before him because he was simultaneously engaged with those things that are, so to speak, unseen. Awareness to the nearness of the Lord will not exempt you from hardship and real-life issues, but it can provide you with the opportunity to be free from the influence of them. Being aware of Jesus' presence in any given situation automatically influences the outcome—and/or response.

It would revolutionize your life if you were more aware of Jesus. Every experience in your life would

INTRODUCTION

be much fuller if you had a constant overwhelming awareness to the nearness of the person of the Lord. There are struggles and challenges that you have been going through, even revolving doors, that will simply fall off of you if you can apprehend what is being presented to you in this moment.

Elisha simply prayed that the Lord would open the eyes of his servant, and God was faithful to do so. I am praying the same prayer that Elisha prayed for his servant for you now. I believe that God will be faithful in the same way. I want you to hold on, because things might never be the same for you.

This spiritual awareness can and will be found through giving yourself over to a lifestyle of fasting. If you are one who is willing to plunge out into the depths of fasting, I encourage you with this: There is a Man, Jesus, who is alive from the dead and now seated at the right hand of the Father, who awaits you out in the deep. He is a wonderful lover, and more good than you realize right now.

Only the truly hungry will fast....

Only the truly hungry will fast....

O Lord, I ask You now to open the eyes of those that walk with You that they might begin to see. Even now Lord, I pray that You awaken their awareness as they give themselves to You in the place of fasting. I pray not a single one would ever be the same. In Jesus' name. Amen!

1

Explanation

Right here, at the beginning of our journey, I believe it would be best to answer two specific questions that will provide the context for moving forward. The two questions are:

1. What is fasting?
2. Why should we fast?

These questions must be answered in order for us to move forward on the same page. Once we are on the same page answering these questions, we will have the proper foundation for a real discussion about fasting and the beautiful walk with Jesus that fasting can help lead us into.

My goal is not to give comprehensive or exhaustive answers in order to win over your intellect. I am going to take, as a college professor of mine would always say, the approach to finding a "Crayola® level" explanation. Jesus said that unless we become like little children, we would not be able to enter the Kingdom.[7]

Many times we feel that if we are going to be "deep" in a subject or an experience that we must also be misunderstood because of our depth. I find it to be quite the opposite. I believe that you can simultaneously be extremely deep and practical. In fact, if you do not possess the ability to break down the high and lofty ideals into simple bite-size pieces, I would argue that you do not really understand for yourself the subject matter you are addressing.

So, in childlike, *not childish*, fashion, let me give a definition of fasting which we will use going forward. Let's start with the definition as a noun:

1. An abstinence from food, or a limiting of one's food, especially when voluntary and as a religious observance.

When used in the tense of a verb, fasting has this definition:

---

[7] Matt. 18:3

Explanation

1. To abstain from all food.
2. To eat only sparingly or certain kinds of food, especially as a religious observance.

From now on, when I speak of fasting I am going to be speaking of it in the way the definitions above engage the term. Fasting is the removal of certain foods, or the abstaining from all food, for a specific period of time, especially as a religious observance. This may cause some issues for certain readers, but that is okay. We will move forward anyway.

These definitions make fasting a pretty straightforward activity. And having a clear definition of what something is means that you immediately also know what it is not. As stated here, fasting is clearly an issue of food and its refusal.

If fasting is about food and only food, then that means fasting is not about television. Fasting is not about social media. Fasting is not about entertainment. Fasting is not about the way that you spend money on certain things, or places you like to go. I understand that there is a tendency in our day to consider other things to be "fasting," but in reality these things are not truly fasting as much as they are disciplines. These other areas of life are disciplinary matters of the mind, body, and even spirit. But they are not fasting. And although fasting can also be a matter of discipline, it is important we not call all matters of discipline a fast.

This might not sit well with you as you are reading, but that is okay. We have to allow the truth to be what it is and then conform our lives to what is true. Truth is not just what we want to be true. Fasting becomes much more palatable when you tell me that I can stay away from watching football for one month and consider it to be sacrificing for Jesus. Fasting is not so bad when you relay it to me in terms of logging out of my Facebook account for two weeks while you let me continue on with life believing that I am going through some grave circumstance for the sake of the Gospel. However, this is not fasting. This should really be called for what it is: practicing self-control and disciplining yourself.

The conversation completely changes when we relate fasting to staying away from certain foods or not eating altogether. The conversation changes because this idea is not something that most people will entertain in our current time and culture. This is not an idea that comes across as being convenient or "easy." It is not supposed to come across as easy because quite frankly, it is not.

Let's take a look at what Jesus has to say about fasting. To best understand and approach fasting it is important we fix our eyes upon the One that matters most, Jesus. In Matthew chapter 6 we find Jesus speaking about three practices that are to be a part of the normal life of someone who is walking with Him and desiring to be more like Him. The three subjects, or practices, that Jesus talks about are giving, prayer, and fasting.[8] Interestingly enough, I find that often these are three areas of great debate for those who walk with Jesus.

Whatever it is that you may believe about these three subjects, I find it telling that in speaking about them Jesus offers no way out. What I mean is, the way that He presents each of the three practices is to say, "*When* you do this…do it this way." This applies to giving: *When* you give. This applies to prayer: *When* you pray. And it also applies to fasting: *When* you fast. "Whenever you fast, do not put on a gloomy face as the hypocrites do, for they neglect their appearance so they will be noticed by men when they are fasting. Truly I say to you, they have their reward in full. But you, when you fast, anoint your head and wash your face so that your fasting will not be noticed by men,

---

[8] Matt. 6:1-18

but your Father who is in secret; and your Father who sees what is done in secret will reward you."[9]

We need to let it fully sink in that Jesus was not offering suggestions here. The thought did not come across as, "Hey, if you ever agree with what I am saying." Or, "Listen guys, if you ever decide that this is going to be easy enough to give your life to." Or, even better, "You know, if you ever decide that you are comfortable with what I am saying, I would suggest that you do it this way." Jesus' words are extremely clear here: *When* you do this means *you will* do this.

There was an expectation on Jesus' part that fasting would be a normal part of life for His followers. Hear that again: Jesus expects that for any and all that follow Him, fasting will be a normal part of your lifestyle. "When you fast, fast like this." He said *when*, not *if*. If we have failed to apply these words from Jesus to our own lives, we are missing out on the beautiful reward that is found only in following Him.

Now, I don't want to take one section of Jesus' words, although it is enough, and make it seem as if that is all that He had to say about it. Let's fast-forward to Matthew chapter 9, and Jesus is being questioned by John's disciples. John's disciples find Jesus and want Him to answer them. Their question is, "How

---

[9] Matt. 6:16-18

is it that we and the Pharisees fast often, but Your disciples do not fast?"[10] Their request seems legitimate. I can understand their frustration. To think that you have given yourself to fasting and prayer and all the while there are some that are walking closely to Jesus without fasting? I can imagine how this would provoke you to approach Jesus with the same line of questioning.

I love Jesus' response to those who questioned Him that day. Jesus says these words, "How can the guests of the bridegroom mourn while he is with them? The time will come when the bridegroom will be taken from them; *then they will fast.*"[11] Then they will fast? Jesus is telling John's disciples that there is a time coming when He will no longer be physically walking beside them on the earth, and when this time comes, those counted as His disciples will be found fasting. Jesus is very direct here about fasting being a part of the life of a disciple after He leaves them. And this isn't where Jesus finishes the discussion about fasting. In fact, there is another place in Matthew chapter 17 where Jesus speaks about fasting again in a very powerful way. We will look more closely into this specific account in the chapter ahead titled "Unbelief."

---

[10] Matt. 9:14
[11] Matt. 9:15 (emphasis added)

Why?

Up until this point we have clearly established as a working definition what fasting is. Let's now look at the question, "Why fast?" The answer is simple: Because Jesus said so. As a follower of Jesus I am committed to the words of Jesus. All of them. It's too easy and totally worthless to take just the bits and pieces that I agree with and fit them into my life.

If fasting is anything, it is this: a posturing of our lives to remain in love with Jesus.

I am always puzzled at the nature of people who choose to try and follow Jesus according to their own plan. No one takes issue with the words of Jesus fitting into their lives when it pertains to some kind of benefit. I don't ever hear anybody trying to come up with an argument as to why God shouldn't bless them. You hardly ever hear about people coming up with a way to prove to you why Jesus shouldn't love them unconditionally or bless them abundantly. Yet when we begin the discussion about fasting, all of a sudden there are all types of red flags, alarms, and points of resistance. There is simply within us something that does not want to have to work for anything in regard to our relationship with Jesus. It is called our flesh. Again, for those who consider that fasting is work,

I wholeheartedly agree that fasting is real work, and hard work at that. Work is a part of following Jesus. In Revelation chapter 2, Jesus has this to say to the church at Ephesus,

> "I know your deeds and your toil and perseverance, and that you cannot tolerate evil men, and you put to the test those who call themselves apostles, and they are not, and you found them to be false; and you have perseverance and have endured for My name's sake, and have not grown weary. But I have this against you, that you have left your first love. Therefore remember from where you have fallen, and repent and do the deeds you did at first; or else I am coming to you and will remove your lampstand out of its place—unless you repent."[12]

Another word for deeds is works. Do the works you used to do at first. First repent, then do the works you used to do in order to keep yourself in love with Me. The issue is not merely applying our lives to works for the sake of working. The goal of our work should be to continually fall deeper in love with Jesus.

---

[12] Rev. 2:2-5

If fasting is anything, it is this: a posturing of our lives to remain in love with Jesus.

Fasting has the power to break the hold of lesser lovers off of our hearts so that we might give more of ourselves to Jesus. In the practice of fasting we are empowered to apply the whole of our affection to the man Christ Jesus. Fasting revives the gaze that has lost its fascination with the Son. Fasting is the means by which a man can relentlessly lock eyes with the ultimate Lover of his soul and not let go. Fasting is both a practice, and a gift given to us, to free our attention from distractions.

The Voice

The most important thing in your life, especially in the area of fasting, is the voice of God. You must live a life that is led. You must develop an internal dependency upon the voice of the Father. In many places in life we come to a place where there is a relentless unwillingness to go deeper and move outside of what we know we have heard, and are hearing, from the voice of the Father. This becomes especially important if you have health concerns that might prevent you at this stage in your life from fasting in the terms we have described. The current condition of your health should always be taken into consideration and paired with practical wisdom in beginning this journey of fasting. Later we will discuss various types of fasting. There are options for fasting when you know you are being invited in and want to exercise wisdom because of your current condition.

With that said, we don't allow practical wisdom to keep us from obeying the voice of

> **Fasting revives the gaze that has lost its fascination with the Son.**

God. The wisdom of this world does not trump the voice of God. We need to be willing to do whatever it is that God is asking us to do. If God is asking you to do it, then He is more than ready, and willing, to provide the grace in order for you to fulfill the invitation. And in situations like this it is important to understand both the Word and character of God—two things He never violates in speaking to us.

This is why we must be a people that are able to recognize and live by the voice of the Father. We must be able to recognize the invitation when it is presented. Without an ear to hear, we will simply try to throw our lives at things that seem to be good, to make sense, or look like they would produce a good outcome. Activities and practices become trial-and-error attempts to capture the hope that we hit the mark somewhere. When led by God, developing a heart to hear His voice, and the ability to obey, there is life in this process. But when we rely on our own ideas, trial and error becomes more like a string of unnecessary mistakes and failures. This is not how it should be for those who are sons and daughters of God. We are to live a life that is led, and led by God Himself.

> **The voice of Jesus will always lead you into places that He desires to walk with you.**

Part of God's character is the reality that the voice of Jesus will always lead you into places that He desires to walk with you. We must remember this simple yet powerful truth. We are not invited into fasting so that we can be abandoned to see how well we do. In fact, it is the exact opposite. We are not able to get the job done, and that is why it takes the empowering presence of Jesus to quicken us to continually obey Him and to be sustained in the place of obedience. This is most important in the place of fasting.

Once you begin, without knowing that you have been invited in by God Himself, there will be a million opportunities and reasons for you to quit at every point and turn as it gets tough. Without a clear sense of direction and purpose in fasting, you will lose the subtle tug-of-war from your flesh in moments of weakness and temptation. And don't think that the enemy simply wants to let you fast. The enemy realizes the powerful breakthroughs that come upon the life of a man or woman who gives themselves to fasting. The enemy's voice will attempt to persuade you to abort your mission, modify your attempt, or conclude your fast before the time is right. Without hearing the voice of the Shepherd clearly, we will falter under the pressure of testing and reason that we have gone far enough. Jesus said that His sheep know His voice and that the voice of another they would not follow.[13] We must be able to discern the voice of Jesus.

Don't continue to follow the voice of your own reason. Don't continue to apply your life to the voice of those who do not see a need for fasting. You do not have to listen to your flesh or the enemy and the presentation of excuses that have been given to keep you out of the beautiful place of experience with God that comes through fasting. The time has come in your life to allow the voice of Jesus to take precedence. And what is the voice of Jesus saying to you? He is saying the same thing that He said to the crowd that day in Matthew chapter 6: "When you fast…do it this way…."

> **The Holy Spirit will always empower you to obey Jesus.**

So far, we have answered the question, "What is a fast?" We have also answered the question, "Why

---

[13] John 10:27

should we fast?" Now it is up to you to determine the answer to the question of *when* it will be that you step into the promises of Christ, with your whole heart, and meet Him in the glorious place of experience. How will you have the ability to fast? The Holy Spirit will always empower you to obey Jesus.

Jesus said it best Himself, "They that love Me will obey Me."[14] Do you love Him? If so, it's time to obey.

---

[14] John 14:15

2

Fascination

The first time that the Bible records a man that goes without eating is found with the life of Moses. This is actually a pretty amazing account in and of itself, and something that stirs me every time I come across it. Let's take a look at the book of Exodus at a time when Moses ascended the mountain to be with God. Exodus chapter 24 gives the incredible story of God meeting with Moses face-to-face, as a man meets with a friend. The exodus, along with all of the struggles to be found in God attempting to bring His people out of the Egyptian captivity and unto Himself, is a place we find the first time a man goes without eating. At the end of chapter 24 we read these words,

"When Moses went up on the mountain, the cloud covered it, and the glory of the Lord settled on Mount Sinai. For six days the cloud covered the mountain, and on the seventh day the Lord called to Moses from within the cloud. To the Israelites the glory of the Lord looked like a consuming fire on top of the mountain. Then Moses entered the cloud as he went up on the mountain. And he stayed on the mountain forty days and forty nights."[15]

There are so many beautiful elements to this story and the way that it is detailed out for us. First, let us start with the understanding that God desired to meet with a man. God's desire is what brought Moses to the top of Mount Sinai. It is key for us to know, and to always remember, that it is because of God's desire for us that we are able to meet with Him. God spoke to Moses and called him unto Himself at the top of the mountain.

The mountain here, for me, represents a clear place of separation. The mountain is a place of being called up and out of the regular rhythms of life. The mountain is a picture of separation from the people and consecration unto God. When Moses applied his will

---

[15] Ex. 24:15-18, NIV

toward climbing the mountain, the glory of God rested upon the top of it in the form of a cloud. A literal cloud descended and rested upon the top of the mountain once Moses arrived at the prescribed place. It was the voice of God that spoke to Moses and called him into the cloud, or the place of meeting. It was there, in the cloud of glory, that Moses met with God for forty days and forty nights.

It is because of God's desire for us that we are able to meet with Him.

I love that the first time fasting is mentioned it is not as some dry, religious, disciplinary action taken by an individual or a group of people in an attempt to prove themselves. I would have hated to see the first mention of someone going without food was because they were attempting to prove they were good enough, strong enough, or religious enough. What I absolutely love is the fact that this account with Moses is actually so far removed from that. This meeting between God and Moses is about a man that was responding in obedience to the voice of God in his life. In hearing and responding, Moses entered into a real place of experience and encounter that transfixed his attention.

Moses' attention was set upon God in such a way that he was not worried about the demands of his flesh and his need for food anymore. Isn't this the way it should be? Shouldn't it be that we can have our fascination with God Himself awakened to the point where we are literally wrapped up in encounters that supersede our natural needs and the demands of our flesh? I would say so. In fact, I would contend for nothing less!

Fascination, by definition, means:

1. To attract and hold attentively by a unique power, personal charm, unusual nature, or some special quality.
2. To arouse the interest or curiosity of.
3. To transfix or deprive of the power or resistance.

Moses, in response to the voice of God, enters the cloud in obedience to meet with Him there. God then holds Moses in an encounter that lasts forty days and forty nights and is able to sustain his natural body without food. This is simply astounding to consider. It is also extremely provoking if you consider all of the implications.

Interestingly enough, God determined the meeting place atop the mountain. God waited for the man He called to make his way to God's determined place before the glory came down and settled there. Please take note: Moses had to climb the mountain to meet with God. Moses had to work his way up the mountain God called him to, and once there, the glory of God came.

There is something about our obedience that attracts the glory of God to settle upon us in a very deliberate way. Obedience to what God was saying brought a life-changing experience with God upon the life of Moses. You can rest assured; God will always meet with a man or woman who is moving in obedience to what He is saying. If this is true, if obedience to the voice of God brings about life-changing experiences with God, then why not simply apply this truth to the practice of fasting? Fasting is a determined place that Jesus has chosen to meet with you. Fasting is a clear-cut place of separation and consecration. Fasting is the cloud that many are not willing to enter into. But to those who are, glory awaits!

In fasting, we find a preoccupation with God that transcends the attention we normally devote to our bodies' regular needs, such as food and all the time and effort food requires. Jesus said it this way when being tempted by the devil himself in the wilderness, "Man shall not live on bread alone, but on every word that proceeds out of the mouth of God."[16] We must

---

[16] Matt. 4:4

realize that the voice and presence of God is enough to sustain us. We truly live by His voice and His presence.

Attention

If fasting is about anything, at a foundational level, it is about attention. Consider with me for a minute how many things are vying for your attention on a regular basis. Think about all of the things that are strategically attempting to win out for the control of your attention. The devil would love nothing more than to keep your mind off of Christ every moment of every day. There is a serious war taking place for our attention to be diverted from the person and presence of God. The prophet Isaiah, in the twenty-sixth chapter of his writing, tells us that God is able to keep in perfect peace those whose minds stay fixed upon Him.[17] Who is God able to keep at perfect peace? The one whose mind is constantly set upon Him. This means that the promise of perfect peace is guaranteed in the place of being able to keep your attention upon God.

Do you want to know why you have an intensified experience with God when you enter into a lifestyle of fasting? It is because your attention is shifted from the normal things in life and set upon

---

[17] Isa. 26:3, ESV

God in a more constant fashion. The reason that God seems to answer more prayers while fasting is because you are actually praying, and praying more than you normally would. The reason that it seems as if God meets you in a greater way while fasting is not because you have found some secret to bring God near. God is always near. It is because you have taken attention that would normally be given to other things and you have set it upon God. Adjusting the issue of your attention has a simply profound effect upon a life lived walking with the Lord.

David, in Psalm 16, says this, "I have set the Lord continually before me."[18] David didn't mean that God would literally come to him in physical form and stand in front of him all the day long. What David is saying is something that is very easy and quite practical for all of us to be able to apply in a life-changing way. David is saying that he determined to keep his attention upon God.

> **If fasting is about anything, at a foundational level, it is about attention.**

We can all make an intentional decision, like David, to continually set the Lord before us. I am not encouraging you to abandon all of your responsibilities. I am not telling you to stop paying attention to

---

[18] Ps. 16:8

things that obviously require you to focus on them day to day. But what I am saying is that attention is more about a posturing of the heart than it is a position of the eyes.

You can remain in the midst of whatever your daily responsibilities may have you doing, all the while you are there in that place having your heart postured before the Lord. This is setting the eyes of your heart upon Him. Regardless of wherever you might find yourself during the day, you can have your mind set upon the Lord. Working a nine-to-five. Sitting in a cubicle. Changing diapers and washing dishes. Working in the kitchen at a restaurant downtown. Regardless of position, remember, attention is about posture.

> **Attention is more about a posturing of the heart than it is a position of the eyes.**

This may seem simple to you, but in all actuality, the substance of what we are discussing here means a world of difference in relationship to experience. Attention brings awareness. The more aware you are of God, the more you are going to interact with Him. Interaction produces exchange, and this is what we are after, divine exchange with the person and presence of God!

3

Objections

Objection: A reason or argument offered in disagreement, opposition, refusal, or disapproval.

It should go without saying; however, I'll say it anyway. Fasting should always be coupled with prayer. Fasting without praying is starving yourself; spiritual dieting at best. Fasting is not an isolated activity. Fasting is not an object unto itself. Fasting, when combined with other disciplines such as prayer, reading the Scriptures, meditation on the Word of God, worship, stillness, and adoration, is one of the revolutionary ways that someone can walk the ancient pathways toward a deeper place of experiential union with Christ.

There are plenty of voices out there that have negative things to say about fasting. We live in a day and age where you can find someone out there preaching and teaching your point of view if you search hard enough. If all you want is someone to stand with you in your current opinions of what life and practice as a believer should be like, you can rest assured there is someone out there to justify you. However, justification in place of accountability and integrity is not a positive. Just because someone will agree with you does not make you right. Since when has agreement with a false opinion ever made that false opinion the truth? You can gather crowds to rally around a lie, but at the end of the day, that lie will never stand before God as truth.

Man's resistance to a truth doesn't change that truth. The stubbornness and hard-heartedness of man doesn't change God. Regardless of the methods we implore to dodge the truth, truth does not change. The truth is rooted in God Himself. The truth is immoveable, and combining half-truths only makes for more tangled lies. Either in life or in judgment, our lives will eventually have to line up. I think the apostle Paul said it best in Romans when he said these words, "Rather, let God be found true, though every man be found a liar."[19]

---

[19] Rom. 3:4

If you have ever had a conversation with someone about fasting, it is quite possible that you have heard some of the things that I also have come across. Comments such as, "Fasting is works," or "You can't fast and get God to do something for you or to give you something." I've been told, "God isn't going to love you more because you are fasting." These are just a few of the things that I personally have heard as I have chosen to give myself to a lifestyle of fasting and prayer. There are plenty more, but there simply isn't enough ink to deal with every silly excuse out there.

As I address some of these frequent objections that come up during conversations about fasting, it is important to note that I am not necessarily talking about unbelievers. We should expect an unbeliever to resist the things of God. I am talking about people who say they love Jesus. Let's start with this one: "You aren't going to get God to love you more by fasting." This is one of my favorites.

I am not looking for God to love me more by giving myself to a lifestyle of fasting. I fast because I know there is *more of me* that needs to love Him. I am very aware that there are hardened places within my own heart and life. As much as I would like to tell you that all of my heart has been completely softened and surrendered, that simply would not be the truth. Smith Wigglesworth said, "There are a thousand areas of my heart that need to be softened a thousand times a day."[20] See, you can fool people. You can even be very impressive to people. However, God knows who you really are and where you are really at.

"You aren't going to change God or get Him to give you something by fasting." This is another good one. Change God? We could never change God. God is unchanged and unmoved by the situations of our lives. God is who He is and will be for all of eternity: past, present, and future. We are not fasting so that we can change God. We give our lives to the practice of fasting so that God can change us! It is not God who needs to be changed; it is you and I.

There is a desperate need in our day for men and women to walk away from excuses. We live in a Christian culture that embraces gray areas, and in doing so, keeps them from the beautiful exchange that awaits us all out in the deep waters of fasting. There is an open door to the Lord that allows Him to work wonderfully in our lives during a time of fasting that is simply not found anywhere else. We are after genuine change, not just external behavioral modification. Fasting drills through the outer core of a man, penetrating all that is supported and kept alive by our flesh,

---

[20] Eric Gilmour, "Meat for Men of God (50 Burning Quotes)," *Voice of Revolution*, August 19, 2011, http://www.voiceofrevolution.com/2011/08/19/meat-for-men-of-god-50-burning-quotes/

and challenges that man in the deepest places of his heart and reality. Fasting provokes, and provides a pathway for the Lord to bring about lasting change.

We also don't fast for stuff. In fact, we don't fast for anything, or anyone, but Jesus. We fast so that we can better posture our hearts and lives to experience His person in a more real way than we currently do. We fast so that we might apprehend Him in a greater way. We fast because there is more of Him to be had. By subjecting the parts of us that tend to self-gratify to starvation, and coupling that with turning toward Jesus, we grow more desperate for Him. There is greater glory to be revealed. There is a place of reward that awaits those who are willing to diligently seek Him.[21]

> **Fasting drills through the outer core of a man, penetrating all that is supported and kept alive by our flesh, and challenges that man in the deepest places of his heart and reality.**

The truth is that I don't have the power in and of myself to break the self-absorbed, self-centered, selfish gaze that so easily settles in my own heart and creeps into my desires. I need the power of the

---

[21] Heb. 11:6

Holy Spirit to loose me of this bondage. It is bondage to be being consumed with, and solely focused upon, myself. Without the help of the Holy Spirit I am left with no one to pursue but myself, and this is captivity of the worst kind.

Another common objection to fasting goes something like this, "You aren't going to get God to do something for you by fasting." This is a really good one, and a statement that I welcome at full speed, as it comes quite frequently. The only thing that I want, and continually stand in desperate need of God doing for me, is breaking the hold of my eyes up and off of my own person so that I might behold Him, as John the Baptist so beautifully said.[22]

We don't fast in order to gain power. We don't fast in order to be granted a greater operation of spiritual gifts. We don't fast so that God can decide to give us more influence. None of these are high enough goals for the place of fasting. All of these lower-level ideals simply don't sparkle bright enough when held up next to the radiance of the person of Jesus. And that is exactly what we do fast for—closeness to the radiant person of Jesus.

We fast for Christ and Christ alone. We fast so that Christ can be formed in us. We fast so that the Father

---

[22] John 1:29

can continue to mold us and make us into the image of His Son, Jesus. We fast so that the expression of our lives might be in alignment with the ways of God. To be godly is to be like God, and this will be impossible in its fullest expression without a lifestyle of fasting. That's right, without a lifestyle of obedient sacrifice, where the most basic physical desires are subjected to the Spirit, we miss out on a certain godliness. Fasting provides a place where we can deny the parts of us that decay and are not eternal and be filled with things of God that will never pass away.

Without the help of the Holy Spirit I am left with no one to pursue but myself.

Plenty of objections support the position as to why fasting may not apply to you. However, though you may be able to develop a lengthy list of *why nots*, there is an amazing *why* that sits at the top of it all and continues to provoke laid-down lovers to go after Jesus. Jesus has determined to meet with you in the lifestyle of fasting. He said as much Himself. Hear it again from me: Jesus is waiting to meet with you in the lifestyle of fasting.

4

Self

I don't think there is any better place to begin this chapter than by looking in the mirror. I believe you are reading this book, at this moment, because you want to take ownership of your life and walk with Jesus. This always begins with looking in the mirror. It will always be easier to blame others for why you are where you are. It will always feel like an easier road to walk when you choose to point the finger at someone or something other than yourself as the reason things are the way that they are in your life. Comparing is an easy out when you compare yourself to people and not Jesus.

Taking ownership means finally putting all of that to an end. Taking ownership means finally disengaging all of that which has really never helped you move forward anyway. Blaming and excuses only give you reason to justify why you aren't where you want to be. Or, more importantly, where your potential in Christ is calling you to go. Taking ownership is making the decision to stop looking at everyone else and to finally stand in front of the mirror and ask yourself, "What must I do?" It is time to own where you are and what you are really going to do about it.

In the third chapter of Philippians, the apostle Paul writes these words, "For many walk, of whom I often told you, and now tell you even weeping, that they are enemies of the cross of Christ, whose end is destruction, *whose god is their appetite,* and whose glory is in their shame, who set their minds on earthly things."[23] These are incredible words written by a father in the Gospel as he is instructing a young body of believers how they ought to live in light of the glorious salvation that has come to them.

Of all the things that Paul decides to write to them, these words are especially intriguing to me because they illustrate a powerful point. "Whose god is their appetite?" What does that actually mean, and why is it something of importance for us to consider as we have set ourselves to walk with Jesus in the power of the Holy Spirit? The language used here paints the picture that these people were consumed with

---

[23] Phil. 3:18-19 (emphasis added)

whatever their appetite desired. These were people whose lives were controlled and led by whatever their appetite demanded in the moment.

Once again, I think it is important that we look at the foundations and establish some basic truths here. We are all made up of three different parts. The three distinct elements to our makeup: we are body, soul, and spirit. The technical, or scientific term in referencing this point we are making would be to say that we are a trichotomy. Our body is the flesh we carry, which Paul, in 2 Corinthians, speaks about as being a tent that we are currently clothed with.[24] Our soul is the place of our mind, the seat of our emotions, the place of our will and ability to make decisions. The book of Proverbs says that the mind of a man plans his way, but the Lord directs his steps.[25] And then lastly, our spirit is that which has been breathed into us by God Himself. Genesis says that in the forming of man God literally breathed into him. God breathed the breath of life into man's nostrils, and it wasn't until then that man became a living being.[26]

These points need to be made so that we can now build a better understanding of what we are. Paul says that their god was their appetite. By definition,

---

[24] 2 Cor. 5:4
[25] Prov. 16:9
[26] Gen. 2:7

an appetite is a desire to satisfy any bodily need or craving. Applying this definition to what Paul is saying in his writing to the Philippians immediately makes things very interesting, to say the least, and gives us a better picture of what is actually being communicated here. So, let's use this definition and look at this portion of the verse one more time with the definition of appetite included: *whose god is their desire to satisfy any bodily need or craving.* This definition changes everything.

You don't need me to convince you that there is a constant fight between your flesh and your spirit. I am sure that you are well aware of the challenges that are to be found here. Paul, in Galatians, tells us that if we will walk in the Spirit we will not gratify the desires of the flesh.[27] It would be ignorance on our part to act as if the flesh doesn't have desires. In fact, I believe that we are all well acquainted with the desires of our flesh. And that's not to say they're all bad.

Some go to great lengths to discipline their flesh in order to minimize or deal with these desires. Some have come up with gimmicks and ways to deal with the flesh that, at best, are nothing more than a hope to suppress those desires long enough to avoid acting upon them. In whatever way that you currently attempt

---

[27] Gal. 5:16, NIV

to manage or manipulate these desires, I can tell you one thing: Without the empowering help of the Holy Spirit in our lives we are doomed to be dominated by our own appetites. We simply do not have what it takes to win the fight against our flesh and its desires in our own strength. Even the most disciplined people are often dominated by desires. The energy they spend on discipline actually indicts them and exposes the power their appetites have over them. In the end, Jesus didn't look at the Pharisees' actions but their heart.[28]

> **Without the empowering help of the Holy Spirit in our lives we are doomed to be dominated by our own appetites.**

The simple truth of what Paul is communicating is that these enemies of the cross were people that could not say no to their fleshly desires, and so the desires controlled their lives. Have you ever felt like this? Have you ever felt overwhelmed with desires that you just could not get a handle on? Have you ever felt defeated about desires that you just could not seem to find a place of victory in? I am sure that you have experienced a moment when what your flesh was asking for was so overwhelming that you caved in.

---

[28] Matt. 15:8-9

Let us now turn our attention back to the mirror for a moment. Maybe at times you are someone that can be included in the group of people that Paul is talking about. I know that the flesh wants to withdraw and even quite possibly be a little offended that such a thing is suggested, but let us examine this a little more. Are you someone that is controlled by the desires of your flesh? Are you someone that has found a way to say no to your flesh when what it wants is seeking to control your life, or your actions in the moment? If we are going to be honest about the situations in our lives, we have to recognize that the reason why most people have not given themselves to the lifestyle and practice of fasting is because they cannot seem to say no to their flesh. Beyond all of what they say they believe, their flesh is what really controls their lives.

Fasting is a declaration of war against your flesh.

You need to understand this: If fasting were easy, everybody would be doing it. The fact is that it is not easy. Fasting is a violent assault against your natural man. Fasting is a declaration of war against your flesh. Fasting pulls back in the tug-of-war that fights to break the hold of your flesh over your mind and spirit.

There is nothing in all of life that will cause your flesh to press the panic button and sound the red alert like the practice of fasting. If you do not believe what I am saying, just go ahead and give it a shot; you will find out really fast what I am saying is true. And for those of you that have practiced fasting, you know the truth of these words.

There is a fight for control in your life. Your flesh, even with your claim to belong to Jesus and all that implies, wants to remain the dominant force in your life. Your flesh wants to remain on top and navigate your life by its desires and cravings. Most have failed to recognize and realize the seriousness of this fight. It is due to a lack of perception, and honestly a claim to willful ignorance that many have chosen in order to continue a "harmless" life of indulgence and comfort rather than obedience and sacrifice.

When was the last time you denied your flesh? When was the last time the Lord spoke to you about not giving in to the cravings of your natural man? I am not talking about blatantly sinful things. There is an immediate tendency to attempt to shift this conversation by applying these questions to obviously immoral and evil things. We aren't talking about how you've been delivered from the greater sin that was in your life before salvation or at a less mature place in your "Christian walk." This is a real question intended to shed light on the subtleties of the flesh and its desire for control in your life. This is a call to go deeper.

Many claim to live a life of empowerment by the Spirit of God. Yet many of these same people cannot, for the life of themselves, step away from the cravings of the flesh when they flare up and demand to be satisfied. Many claim to walk in the power of the Spirit but can't seem to muster up enough of that power to turn the television off and put their attention upon Jesus. Why do we claim to be hungry for God while we can't turn aside from the table and deny ourselves a meal to be with Him?

Fasting restores hunger in your life.

Only the truly hungry will fast!

You need to understand that there is power in fasting that breaks the hold of the flesh. There is an induced weakness in fasting that cripples the strength of the flesh and its dominance over our lives. By fasting, and the learning of utter dependence upon God to sustain us, we will begin to confront certain controlling factors over our lives that we never knew existed and have been allowed to remain.

Fasting alone breaks you from the locked position of fixation with yourself. Fasting destroys pride in your life and helps to bring you low. Fasting utterly does away with the mind-set that you are in complete control of your life. There is nothing like fasting that will cause you to realize the deception of your flesh. Fasting is an invitation to a freedom that is from the

Lord and tears you away from the manipulative control of the flesh and its cravings.

It takes a simple childlike belief in Jesus to think that you can be sustained physically, emotionally, and spiritually for any amount of time without giving in to your flesh to live and be happy. You really have to be foolish, in a way, to think you can live for extended periods of time without feeding yourself with anything other than contact with Jesus. This is exactly the point. Your flesh will attempt to persuade you with a wisdom that will lead you away from the fasting that God is inviting you into. In fact, your flesh will tell you all sorts of crazy things to get you not to fast.

In your battle against your flesh, and don't forget it is a battle, do not think for one minute that your flesh is just going to lay down and die. There must be an awareness on your part that it is going to require something more in your life than the simple desire to win out here. Desire will never be enough. Discipline alone will not be enough either. Fasting restores hunger in your life. There is nothing in the entire world that has the power to jumpstart your appetite for God like fasting. Fasting is the catalyst to a burning heart. By emptying yourself, fasting provides empowerment for your eyes to remain fixed upon the Lord, and not just your own desires.

There are those who will put forth a valiant effort in an attempt to suppress desires that they have not been able to overcome by discipline. This is one of the key problems with discipline alone: you don't deal with the desire; you only sweep it under the rug and deal with surface areas of your life. Discipline without dealing with desire is just suppression. Suppression does not equal victory. These strongholds don't need to be suppressed; they need to be evicted. Fasting serves the eviction notice.

Give yourself to fasting. Push away the plate to spend time in adoration. Then, turn off the television and be with Jesus. Set your eyes upon the Lord in the place of fasting and watch as the hold that has always kept you captive to your own cravings diminishes. Begin running to Jesus in the direction of fasting and never look back. Let this echo in your heart! You do not have to be controlled by your appetite. Your flesh does not always have to have the final say. You do not have to continue to make sacrifices at the altar of your cravings. There is a wonderful place of freedom for you once the god of your flesh has been evicted. Fasting is the place where your flesh is judged and the Spirit empowers you to enforce the verdict.

5

Habit

Habit

1. An acquired behavior pattern regularly followed until it has become almost involuntary.
2. A dominant or regular disposition or tendency: prevailing character or quality.
3. Mental character or quality.

Physical hunger is something that is easy to focus on when entering into fasting. You know you will get hungry at some point, and these are moments you will have to be willing to battle through in order to keep moving forward. However, let me encourage you with something: Hunger is the easy part of the fight. Yes, it is true. Hunger is not the real struggle when fasting.

Understand, I am not overlooking the fact that your flesh gets hungry. I am not for one minute downplaying the reality that you are carrying flesh and that it is going to get overwhelmingly hungry when you stop feeding it. This is an honest fight when giving yourself to fasting. And for some the challenge is greater than for others. But the real struggle in a fast will be against habit.

Physical hunger is easier to crush than habit.

In the process of fasting, physical hunger is easier to crush than habit. It must be understood that not all hunger is bad. Hunger is a result of the biological way we are formed by God. It is permanent. It is powerful. It is there for a reason. However, as powerful as physical hunger is, it is supposed to be subordinate to our mind. It is intended, by God's design, that our mind has control over our body's desires, physical hunger being one. Greater than the mind's control over the body, the spirit is designed to be superior to the mind. The spirit that is united to God is to be the dominating factor of our makeup.

Physical hunger in relation to food and how it affects fasting deals a momentary affliction to your flesh. Even though some of those moments will seem like an eternity, they are still just moments. Momentary struggles. Momentary fights. Habits that have been developed over time in relationship to food, on the other hand, deals with your natural disposition. Habit deals with the things you are subconsciously doing that you don't even necessarily realize anymore because they have become such an ingrained part of who you are. I would like for you to see it this way: Hungry is something that you get from time to time; habit is something that you have become.

Knowing the difference in the two of these terms and how they apply can bring powerful changes in the way you approach fasting. Again, physical hunger is much easier to crush than habit. Over the process of time, when fasting, and especially charting out into deep waters of extended fasting, the period of physical hunger will go. You will reach places in extended fasting where your physical hunger will actually subside and no longer be an issue. But when your physical hunger dissipates, the habits you've developed over time in your relationship with food will remain.

Hungry is something that you get from time to time; habit is something that you have become.

In the fourth chapter of John's gospel, John tells of an interaction that takes place between Jesus and a woman from Samaria at a well in the middle of the day. This meeting between Jesus and the Samaritan woman presents us with a picture of empowerment that deals directly with habits. Let's look at the Scripture as it unfolds after Jesus arrives at the well,

> "There came a woman of Samaria to draw water. Jesus said to her, 'Give Me a drink.' For His disciples had gone away into the city to buy food. Therefore, the Samaritan woman said to Him, 'How is it that You, being a Jew, ask me for a drink being that I am a Samaritan woman?' (For Jews have no dealings with Samaritans.) Jesus answered and said to her, 'If you knew the gift of God, and who it is who says to you, "Give Me a drink," you would have asked Him, and He would have given you living water.' She said to Him, 'Sir, you have nothing to draw with and the well is deep; where then do You get that living water? You are not greater than our father Jacob, are You, who gave us the well, and drank of it himself and his sons and his cattle?' Jesus answered and said to her, *'Everyone who drinks of this water will thirst again; but whoever drinks of the water that I will give him shall never thirst*; but the water that I will give him will become in him a

well of water springing up to eternal life.' The woman said to Him, 'Sir, give me this water, so that I will not be thirsty nor come all the way here to draw.'"[29]

I think it is important to simplify what is happening in this text before we venture any further. Jesus is resting by a well and His disciples have gone into town to buy food after a long day. While resting, a woman from the nearby town of Samaria approaches the well. As she comes to draw water, which she most likely would have done once every day, Jesus asks her for a drink. But His request catches the woman off guard because of the cultural divides and social barriers of their day. This interaction is man to woman, Jew to Samaritan; and these were lines which came with distinct implications.

Even as Jesus crossed those cultural barriers, the woman enters into the discussion with Him. Jesus tells her about a spiritual drink that He is able to offer to her that would eliminate the deepest thirst within her. Jesus uses her need for the continued trips to the well as a living illustration. This woman, lacking spiritual awareness, is excited about the thought of no longer having to make the journey to the well and says to

---

[29] John 4:7-15 (emphasis mine)

Jesus, "Sir, give me this water, so that I will not have to come all the way here to draw."[30]

Now the stage is set; let me simplify even more. Jesus is standing next to a natural well, yet He is speaking of receiving a drink from another well with water powerful enough, and satisfying enough, to cause this woman to never thirst again. This woman, without a clear understanding of what is happening in the moment, is now face-to-face with the well that never runs dry. This woman from Samaria is standing in front of the One, who in and of Himself, is the river of living water. The offer that Jesus makes to this woman, as simple as it may seem, has powerful implications for us today as He issues the very same invitation to you and me.

Remember that taking the daily journey to the well in order to satisfy her thirsts would have been a regular part of her life. As this woman thirsted, and lacked water to fulfill her needs, she would journey to the well in order to make provision for that very thirst rising up in her life. This natural well would have been a place of provision. This well would have been a place of necessity for her and many others. It is no different for you today.

---

[30] John 4:15

Let's now connect the dots between the natural well and the offering of freedom that Jesus presents the Samaritan woman, which comes from the spiritual well not seen with natural eyes. Jesus is contrasting the natural wells of life with coming to Him, who is our spiritual well. Jesus juxtaposes Himself against the natural wells we draw from daily which seem to offer momentary satisfaction, yet always leave us thirsting again. As Jesus stands next to the natural well, He offers her a drink of Himself.

It is no different for you and me. Jesus stands next to the "natural wells" that you have learned to rely on and are now bound to. He stands there waiting and offers you the opportunity to draw from Him and truly be free. Jesus sees the journey that you continue to make day by day to the natural wells of life and how you have become fatigued and worn out from your endless need to return to them. It is in this place that Jesus stands and opens the door for you to freedom!

I need to emphasize that the connection Jesus makes between our natural need for water and the freedom that only comes through Him is extremely significant. We know that there is a very real and very powerful connection between food and the systems of the body. That is natural since food provides the body the fuel it needs to run those systems. But have you ever made the connection to your emotions? Have you ever noticed that depending on what is happening in your life, or how your day is going, you can actually be influenced and driven toward the desire for certain foods that make you feel better rather than just provide you energy? It is quite funny, but yet a very appropriate coincidence, that the word desserts is just the word stressed spelled backwards!

As funny as that might be, the truth still remains. We are prone to lean towards certain types of food depending on how we are feeling in a given moment. Why is this? I have asked myself that very same question. However, I did not just stop at asking the question. I wanted a real answer. This is what I found.

Chemical Warfare

I am sure that you are familiar with the term aphrodisiac. If not, by definition an aphrodisiac is a food, drug, potion, or other agent that arouses sexual desire. Let's look more intently into an aphrodisiac and its relationship specifically to food. What types of foods make it to this list? Oysters, chili peppers, chocolate, avocados, bananas, honey, coffee, watermelon, chai tea, pine nuts, arugula, figs, olives and olive oil, strawberries, artichokes, pomegranates, cherries, pumpkin seeds, and whipped cream, just to name a few.[31] This is a long list of "aphrodisiac" foods; however, there are many more. These foods have not been legitimized by the FDA, but are said to promote sexual desires in many cultures and by many leading experts.

In light of this, it is interesting to consider that during consumption of certain foods, many on the list just provided, there is a spike in dopamine in the body. Dopamine has been identified as the body's reward center, controlling the pleasure center of our brain.[32] An increase in dopamine heightens feelings of euphoria, empathy, and love, as well.

So what exactly are we talking about here and why am I pointing out aphrodisiacs and their relationship to food? I want you to see that there is a chemical process triggering deeper responses. There is activity taking place within your body that is not visible to you and it is having a profound effect on why you are doing what you are doing. Science now acknowledges a human condition of bondage called food addiction.

This is very important in our journey to being spiritually free. Have you ever considered you might be subject to this bondage? Food addiction is a real

---

[31] Alyssa Jung, "19 Aphrodisiac Foods Proven to Spark Romance," *Reader's Digest,* http://www.rd.com/food/fun/aphrodisiac-foods/.

[32] Quentin Shires, Instructor, "What is Dopamine? – Definition & Function," *Study.com,* http://study.com/academy/lesson/what-is-dopamine-definition-function.html.

condition. Food addiction can "manifest itself in the uncontrollable craving for excess food that follows the ingestion of refined carbohydrates, primarily sugars and flour substances that are quickly metabolized and turned into sugar in the bloodstream."[33]

Most people that end up in some sort of addiction did not necessarily sit down and decide that they wanted to become an addict. The same is very true for individuals who end up in food addiction—people don't choose to lose total control of their eating. Instead there are factors that "help" the process along and can result in the descent into addiction.[34]

When you eat starches and sweets, your pancreas releases insulin. In addition to regulating your blood sugar, insulin also decreases your blood stream concentration of amino acids—except for tryptophan. Eventually the tryptophan makes its way to your brain and triggers it to produce serotonin (your feel-good chemical). Then you get that soothing, calming sensation you're seeking. In addition, refined carbohydrates also trigger increased releases of the neurotransmitters dopamine and norepinephrine, and as your brain becomes flooded with these chemicals, you can get a

---

[33] "The Truth About Carbohydrate Addiction (And What To Do About It)," *Healthy Holistic Living*, http://www.healthy-holistic-living.com/the-truth-about-carbohydrate-addiction-and-what-to-do-about-it.html?t=JERF.

[34] Ibid.

feeling of euphoria...then crave more refined carbs as a result![35]

I hope that you are able to see exactly what we are getting at here. You have to realize that your drive towards certain foods is based on more than the fact that you love the way that certain things taste. Sure, taste is a big motivator, but it is not all that is happening.

There is also the feeling you experience by consuming certain things. This is how you get the term comfort foods. They are called comfort foods because they give you a comforting feeling. There is a certain satisfaction that your body receives by eating certain things. So, you are actually becoming addicted to the satisfaction, or the feeling, that you get from eating different foods. You need to make the connection between the food and what is happening in your system. Until you do this you will always return to the natural well Jesus stood next to in John chapter 4.

Maybe your go-to food is sweets. Maybe you crave carbs. Some crave salty stuff. Whatever it is in your case, we have to wake up and see the truth of what

---

[35] "The Truth About Carbohydrate Addiction (And What To Do About It)," *Healthy Holistic Living,* http://www.healthy-holistic-living.com/the-truth-about-carbohydrate-addiction-and-what-to-do-about-it.html?t=JERF.

is actually happening. We need to be able to recognize the pull towards certain foods that make us feel a certain way. We need to understand that this is not just random. This isn't just some myth either. There is a very real reason why.

You see, regardless of what your well is, Jesus wants to be what satisfies you. Jesus patiently waits by the well that you run to on a daily basis, or in your times of need, and watches as you consume whatever it is that you believe will quench that thirst within you. Jesus is waiting for you to realize the bankruptcy of your efforts. Jesus is hoping that today would be the day that you would take Him up on His offer of freedom. Being free from the physical, emotional, and spiritual grip food has on us is a key to this experience.

Jesus told the woman from Samaria, "If you would drink the water that I give, you would never thirst again."[36] These words are extremely powerful when you hear them in light of what we have been discussing. These words hold tremendous weight in relation to the opportunity that Jesus is giving to you to be free from natural wells, which often become addictions and bondage.

---

[36] John 4:14

Too often bread alone wants to be our satisfaction. Am I saying Jesus was calling the woman to a fast? No. But I am saying that Jesus was calling her to a place of freedom and life, which He has prepared for all of us. He was calling her to Himself, to the well of living water, to the bread of life. Jesus is the sole person and place where we can be completely satisfied, even beyond physical satisfaction. You and I are not the Samaritan woman at Jacob's well with Jesus, but you and I can partake of Jesus the same as she could. Fasting readies our hearts to feast on things from above.

You see, regardless of what your well is, Jesus wants to be what satisfies you.

Fasting enables you the opportunity to confront the "other" satisfactions that sell us short of the heavenly feast. Fasting allows you the privilege to choose Jesus over your body. Choosing Jesus in times of fasting is about more than simply not eating. Fasting is not just a turning from food, as it is sometimes deemed. Fasting is a "turning from," but it is equally, and if not more importantly, "a turning to." We turn from food and turn to Jesus!

If all you are doing during times of fasting is turning from food without turning to Jesus, you are missing the entire point. The offer of freedom isn't given to those who simply find a way to not come to the natural well anymore. The offer of freedom from the thirsts and hungers that have controlled your life is found within the invitation to come to Jesus. Jesus is our comforter. Jesus is our satisfier. Jesus is where we should run in times of need.

Below the Radar

Fasting will bring you face-to-face with the knowledge of certain habits that Jesus wants to deal with in your life. During a short fast it is easier to just bury these habits and never have to contend with them at any point. When fasting for a day or a few days you can most likely go unchallenged in some areas of habit. However, when you venture into consistent and longer periods of fasting, these habits will eventually be exposed. Unavoidable habits of bondage will stand out in the middle of your pathway like a fork in the road demanding you to choose how to proceed.

On shorter stints of fasting, habits actually have the potential to just lay low and fly below the radar. Even during seasons of spiritual highs, great energy, and seeming determination in these areas, habits fly according to the pace of life and go unnoticed. When a habit goes unnoticed, it remains unchallenged. A habit that never gets directly challenged will never be dealt with. We must be diligent in these matters. There must be a real acknowledgment of the battle for who we are. Once that battle is understood, it can be approached with more than just a casual "maybe one day" attitude. Have you ever asked the Lord what things are currently satisfying you outside of His person and His presence?

Maybe you would be intimidated to ask such a thing because of what may be revealed to you. Or maybe you already know and you have just been avoiding the head-on confrontation with these other lesser "wells." Whichever category you find yourself in, the time is now to be free. The offer of freedom stands before you, if you are willing to walk into it. Jesus wants to be what you turn to in your moments of need. Jesus waits for us to realize His presence and His all-sufficiency. He really is an endless well with the power to satisfy the thirst of your heart. You can turn to Jesus, and in your turning, find the empowerment to break free from the attachments to lesser wells.

> **A habit that never gets directly challenged will never be dealt with.**

6

Unbelief

Unbelief: The state or quality of not believing; incredulity or skepticism, especially in matters of doctrine or religious faith.

Matthew chapter 17, as briefly touched on earlier, tells the special story which will help us to understand the nature and consequence of unbelief. The characters are Jesus, the disciples, the father of a demonized young man, and that young man controlled by demonic forces. Jesus and the disciples have just come down from an extraordinary encounter on the top of the mountain where Jesus literally transfigured before the three of them. As Jesus was glorified, Moses and Elijah appeared alongside Jesus, and the voice of the Father spoke audibly for even those disciples to hear.

Returning from the mountaintop, they are confronted by a crowd of people. A father whose son is constantly battling seizures approaches Jesus. In an attempt to describe his son's condition to Jesus, the father says, "He often falls into the fire and often into the water. I brought him to your disciples but they couldn't heal him." There is a sense of frustration in Jesus' response to this father. Jesus says, "You unbelieving and rebellious generation! How long will I be with you? How long must I put up with you? Bring him here to me."[37] The Bible tells us that Jesus rebukes the demon out of the boy, and that from that moment, the boy was healed and brand new. What happens next is what I would like to focus on in this chapter. Jesus' disciples approach Him privately to ask Him the question, "Why couldn't we drive [the demon] out?"[38]

Let's look at Jesus' response in its entirety, "Because of your lack of faith," He told them. "For I assure you: if you have faith the size of a mustard seed, you will tell this mountain, 'Move from here to there,' and it will move. Nothing will be impossible for you. However, *this kind does not come out except by prayer and* fasting."[39]

---

[37] Matt. 17:15-17, HCSB
[38] Matt. 17:19, HCSB
[39] Matt. 17:20-21, HCSB (emphasis added)

I love the fact that the disciples were bothered that their life and efforts didn't seem to produce the result they thought they should have. I also love the fact that they did not just sit around in their frustration or their lack of answers. The disciples went to Jesus, in private, and wanted to get some sort of resolve to their embarrassing "issue." They are doing exactly what I would hope any of us would do if we were in the same situation.

After all, it was obvious by their experience they didn't have an answer. The Word says the father took his son to Jesus' disciples, yet they were not able to do anything for him. But how could this be? What could have made the effort lack the results that Jesus was able to get when He rebuked the demon from the young boy? Hadn't they learned how to deal with these exact situations by watching Jesus?

We can find clarity by looking at the way that Jesus chooses to respond to the private question posed by the disciples. Jesus says to them that they lack faith; they didn't see the desired result of their actions because they had a lack. Could it be possible you are suffering the same condition? Or, maybe the reason your life is not producing is because the faith you think you have is not actually functioning in the power it should. But is it possible there is a disconnect between what you are doing and what you are believing?

A lack of faith? How can that be? Sometimes it's easy to admit our own lack, but the disciples walked side by side with Jesus! In defense of the disciples, I am sure that they were just trying to do what they had seen Jesus do many times. I am convinced that they must have known the right actions to take in that given situation; Jesus had been healing, delivering, and even raising the dead. Clearly their issue was not simply with activity or the movement of religious activity. They knew the right way to go about doing what they were attempting to do.

But even though they had the right activities in place, they just weren't seeing the results. What they knew and expected wasn't producing what they thought they should. This is why they approached Jesus and asked the ever-so-important question, "Why couldn't we do it?" Jesus meets them head-on in their quest for understanding. I don't know if they were ready for the truth of what Jesus' answer revealed to them.

Jesus doesn't just leave the disciples in a hopeless situation. After revealing their lack, He actually provides the answer to how they could fill the gap. The last words of Jesus' response are powerful. Jesus finishes His answer with words that have been hotly debated, and in fact, have even been removed from some newer translations of the Bible. Jesus says, "This kind does not come out except by prayer and fasting."

This kind? What kind? Remember, Jesus answered them after indicting them for lacking faith. Before He gives them the answer to their problem, He reveals why they aren't seeing the results they expect from their "doing." A lack of faith, in other words, is a lack of belief. A lack of belief is unbelief. What Jesus is pointing out here is crucial for us to understand.

Understand, the issue wasn't that they didn't know what to do; they had this part down. The crux of the issue was not a matter of activity, but believing in the One whose power is key to any activity bearing real fruit. At the heart of all that you do and say must be a belief in Christ that gives substance to your actions and words. If not, what you will continually find is hollow actions and words that lack results. Faith in our actions and ourselves isn't able to produce simply because it is rooted in our own actions and power and not the faith that Jesus is the One acting in power through us.

> **At the heart of all that you do and say must be a belief in Christ that gives substance to your actions and words.**

Let's boil this down even more. Point blank, Jesus is telling the disciples, "I know that you guys have the right motions. That's not the problem. The real problem is not what you are doing. The real problem is that there is deeply embedded unbelief in your heart that is crippling the efforts of your life." We have to understand that in many situations we find ourselves in the exact same place that the disciples were in. Just having a head knowledge of what to do in a given circumstance is not what gets the job done—not when walking with Jesus. We must be those who actually believe with our hearts in Christ and His power if we desire to see results.

Interestingly, Jesus was confronted by the Pharisees and scribes just a short time before this interaction with the disciples. Among the things spoken, what sticks out is Jesus' words found in Matthew chapter 15, verse 8, "These people honor Me with their lips, but their heart is far from Me."[40] Wow! They were saying something with their lips that was not being fully engaged and backed with belief in their hearts. Just as it was in the situation with the disciples and the demon-possessed boy, what matters most is not always what is visible on the surface. The Pharisees and scribes were society's best religious models. They knew the Scripture and the law better than anyone. But their activity and knowledge was the foundation of their faith, not Jesus Himself.

Whatever the situation may be, when we continually give our life to practices and activities that we

---

[40] Matt. 15:8, HCSB

expect to bring certain results but our experience falls short, we should learn to come to a private place with Jesus and ask the very same question that the disciples did. We need to ask the Lord, "Why can't I do it?" We must learn to find a place alone with Jesus, away from the crowd, and seek the reasons why our life is not producing what He says it should. The question, "Why can't I do it?" will always remain the same. Have you ever asked Jesus this question? Has any part of your life ever not lined up with what Jesus said it should look like? If you are like most of us, the answer is yes.

I love that in dealing with the disciples, Jesus doesn't just rebuke them, but He provides a bridge. I have learned that in correction and teaching Jesus usually offers a way that I am able to cross in order to lay hold of the desires of my heart. He doesn't just solve the problem, but He offers us to walk through the process with Him.

Back in the story, Jesus speaks to their lack of faith and says that, "this kind can only come out by fasting and prayer." And so it is with you and me. There are certain places of unbelief that lie within your heart that you are not aware of right now that can only be confronted and conquered through prayer and fasting. And prayer and fasting, by definition, involves intimate time in closeness with Jesus.

What do I mean when I say that there are places of unbelief you are not aware of right now? Well, let's look back at the situation with the disciples. They were going through the motions and obviously didn't realize that unbelief contained within their hearts was preventing them from experiencing the fullness of their relationship with Jesus in praying the demon be cast out. There was unbelief which had taken up residence in their hearts that they didn't know was living there. Ultimately this unbelief allowed the demon, or this specific challenge, to overcome them.

Prayer and fasting is the pathway to revealing and overcoming hidden places of unbelief in our heart and life.

This begs the question: How do I deal with unbelief that I don't even know that I have? Once again, it's Jesus' words that give us hope. Prayer and fasting is the pathway to revealing and overcoming hidden places of unbelief in our heart and life. Well, isn't there some other way? That seems a little extreme, don't you think? The word *only* that Jesus includes in His response to the disciples lets us know that it will *only* be by praying and fasting that this confrontation is possible.

There is an opportunity to meet with Jesus in the place of fasting that makes the unraveling of our hearts possible. There is a meeting with Jesus in the place of fasting where He is able to free us from certain entanglements. Unbelief is a major one of those entanglements. We have to see, that in the practice of fasting, what is not visible becomes visible and what is unknown becomes known. Fasting is a means by which Jesus is able to purify your heart and life by revealing issues that might otherwise remain buried.

There are certain deadly toxins, unbelief being one, that lie dormant within your heart. These deadly toxins, such as unbelief and many others, can be confronted and conquered through the process of prayer and fasting. These toxins must be purged. These toxins must not be allowed to remain as residents in our heart. If these toxins are not dealt with, it will not matter what activities you have in place in your life. You will continually be faced with the frustration the disciples experienced that day as they attempted to deliver the boy from the demon. Fasting can purge the heart. Fasting can realign your heart with the belief that it is Christ in you working His power through you.

Keep in mind; the issue is not one of deliverance for others. It is clear that Jesus was not encouraging the disciples in how they could just be better at driving out demons. What Jesus was after was His disciples being delivered from the unbelief that kept them from living in the full experience of all that He made available to them. He desires the same for us. There has to be substance that backs our words and activities. This substance is secured in the place of believing.

Let it never be said of you, as it was the Pharisees, that though you praise Him with your lips, your heart is distant. Though you lay hands on the sick, your heart is far from Him. Though you attend services and seem to be involved in your church, your heart is distant. Because if you claim that He loves you and you really don't believe, your words and life will lack the substance which comes as the result of true belief.

Fasting is a means by which Jesus is able to purify your heart and life.

Don't allow unbelief to remain in your life. Jesus has provided us with a glorious solution! Prayer and fasting is glorious when we realize what it produces in us. Seek Jesus in the place of prayer and fasting and ask Him to reveal to you the areas of your own heart and life that have been reduced to motion without substance. Ask Him to show you the things in your own heart and life that have stood in your way as a hindrance to fully living in the experience of all that has been made available to you.

If you are faithful to meet Him in the way that He has prescribed, namely prayer and fasting, He is faithful to root out those hidden toxins in your heart.

There is not one of us that wants to live a life of unbelief. You don't want to be one that knows what you should say or what you are supposed to do yet doesn't believe deeply enough that the experience is yours to be had. I know you don't. And neither do I.

Read these words again, "This kind will only come out by prayer and fasting." I pray that you would allow this reality to rest upon your life as you adventure into prayer and fasting with the Holy Spirit. I know He will clearly and powerfully reveal Jesus to you. Don't allow unbelief to continue to cripple the efforts of your life one more day.

More Than You Can Bear

In John chapter 16 Jesus is talking with the disciples about future situations that they will encounter once He has left the earth. He is speaking to them very plainly about their future. In verse 12 we find words from Jesus that I want you to see. Jesus says, "I have many more things to say to you, but you cannot bear them now."[41] There was obviously much more that Jesus could have revealed to them before He left them, but He chose not to. He didn't reveal to them all that He could have because He said they couldn't bear it at the time. There was something about the limitations

---

[41] John 16:12

to their current capacity that would not allow Jesus to continue in what He was releasing to them.

What I have found to be true in my own life is that unbelief has directly influenced what Jesus was willing to speak to me in different seasons of my life. Jesus is not interested in wasting words with me. In fact, Jesus never wastes words. What He says He means, and He means it more than we are willing to realize or believe at times. Scripture says that He regards His word even higher than His name.[42] It is when I am incapable of bearing His words that Jesus often holds them back.

There is so much that Jesus desires to tell us. He is endless, and therefore there is more to His voice and the things that He wants to talk about with you. If there is a quiet or a lack of hearing in your life, don't attribute it to an unwillingness to speak on Jesus' part. At times we will find ourselves in the exact same spot that the disciples found themselves in this area. There is so much that Jesus wants to say. Often there just isn't a capacity on our end to handle what He has to say.

How does this relate to fasting? Great question. There will be seasons of your life where God will not be able to talk about certain things because of the unbelief that has taken up residency in your heart. Because of this unbelief, if He were to speak about

---

[42] Psalm 138:2, ESV

certain things, they would simply fall to the ground because you would not be willing to believe them. Or worse, they would crush us under the weight of their implications.

Have you ever heard something from God or felt something in your spirit that was unbelievable? Has God ever revealed something to you that you thought was absolutely crazy? I'm talking about something so wild and distant in nature from your current place in life at the time He spoke it that you just couldn't bring yourself to face or embrace it? This is a hint of what I am talking about.

Unbelief hinders us from seeing the fullness of all that God is saying. It is not that God lacks faithfulness; it is that we lack belief.

Or how about this. Have you ever heard something from the Lord, and you knew you heard from God, but because you could not really believe it you decided to take it to someone close to you to see what they thought? Then, when the report from that person did not come back favorable, or they just did not want to see God do it in your life, you decided to walk away from the word of the Lord?

There are many words that have fallen to the ground and been walked away from because of a lack of belief on our part. Unbelief hinders us from seeing the fullness of all that God is saying. It is not that God lacks faithfulness; it is that we lack belief. We are on our way to an increase in capacity once unbelief in our hearts has been confronted and conquered. Increased capacity means an increase in what Jesus is able to say to us.

Sometimes we won't even struggle with what God has to say, but we hold unbelief about His intentions and character. There are times God tells His kids things which seem difficult, but our inability to believe in His goodness, His faithfulness, and His dedication to seeing His word fulfilled prevents us from being able to bear those words. This is just as critical as actually being able to believe what He is saying. If God wants to trust us with certain things, we must first trust God's intentions and ability to fulfill everything He says.

Simple childlike faith and belief is the womb of miracles.

There will be specific times and seasons where Jesus will lead you into fasting because there is something that He has to say to you that He doesn't want you to miss. In this way the discipline of fasting is actually a gift of God's grace. In these times and seasons He will have to lead you out into fasting so that the unbelief that would have stood in your life and hindered you could be dealt with.

In fasting, God is creating for you a clear pathway to hear what He is saying by reinforcing our belief in Him. This is a path clear of many fleshly distractions, and a path that teaches us more about Him. As we learn to hear and obey in fasting, we will come to know a greater trust in the One who carries us through the dying that fasting brings us into. Fasting draws us near to Him by shattering so many of the barriers that hinder our faith.

Again, we must not forget that God is not after wasting His voice with us. After all, if He speaks things we cannot handle or perceive correctly, we can be disappointed or broken and our faith ultimately eroded. Jeremiah chapter 1 tells us that God jealously watches over His word waiting to perform it.[43] Once He speaks He is more ready to fulfill His word then we are to believe it.

If we let Him, He will lead us into fasting because it is here that He can sever the tie with unbelief that has hindered His word to us in the past. He will lead us into fasting to free us so that we might be able to bear all that He has to say to us. He will lead us into fasting so that our own wisdom won't stand in the way and cause us to question rather than embrace what He is about to say. He will lead us into fasting because this is

---

[43] Jer. 1:12

where we return to the place of enough childlike dependency and simply respond as Mary. When Gabriel told her what God wanted to do in her life, "May it be done to me according to your word,"[44] was her reply. Simple childlike faith and belief is the womb of miracles, just as it was in Mary's case. Childlike faith is a simple belief that whatever God says, He is able to do.

Allow God to destroy unbelief in your life through fasting.

What could God say to you right now if unbelief were not in the way? This is a question that should drive you into the secret place to cry out for the removal of all that would hinder His voice to you! The thought of there being more that God would talk to you about should posture your heart before Him in such a way to jealously desire the removal of all obstacles in your life. Allow God to destroy unbelief in your life through fasting. Give yourself to Him in the place of fasting and prayer and purify your heart from the deadly unbelief that so easily takes up residence within. Grab ahold of Jesus in fasting and get ready for the extraction of all that would hinder His voice in your life.

---

[44] Luke 1:38

7

Deliverance

I would like to share an experience with you that I had seven years ago. Up until now it has only been shared with a handful of people. I was close to the completion of my very first forty-day liquid fast. It was September 3, 2009, the day I was concluding the fast. It is a day that I will forever remember. My wife was pregnant at the time with our soon-to-be first-born little girl. She was seven months pregnant to be exact. We were youth pastoring at a local church in Central Florida. I was a student at a university nearby working on my undergraduate degree in theology. We were much younger then and did whatever we felt led to bring Jesus the maximum amount of glory with our lives.

It was drawing towards the end of the workday at the church office, and knowing this would be the night that I would close the fast, I wanted to spend some time in prayer and worship by myself before heading home. I decided to withdraw into the room where our youth ministry gathered weekly. There I sat down on the floor of the altar with my full attention on Jesus. I sensed such an overwhelming closeness to Jesus in those moments. There is something special about fasting that softens our hearts and resensitizes our lives to the voice and presence of Jesus. In silent adoration I set my gaze upon the Lamb.

I felt a prompting in my heart to ask the Lord what the significance of forty days is all about. I mean, why not forty-two, why not thirty-seven? I know that forty in the Scriptures is representative of a generation. There are many places that we could prove this point, but the clearest is found in Exodus. In Exodus, God allows forty years to pass and a generation of people to die before moving forward into the Promised Land.[45] As I sat, lost in the moment with only the Lord and my questions, I heard the still, soft voice of the Holy Spirit from within say words to me that have forever changed my life. The Holy Spirit said to me, "You have repaired the breach." Even as I write these words it brings tears to my eyes. I did not really understand

---

[45] Num. 14:22-23

what was being said to me in the moment. My only response was to ask, "Lord, what does that mean?"

I don't know any other way to explain to you what happened other than to simply tell it just as it unfolded. For those of you who see prophetically or who understand the gift of seeing, this might not be so troubling. To the rest, I pray that the Lord Himself would teach you to see and that it would forever change the way you experience and walk with Him.

There is something special about fasting that softens our hearts and resensitizes our lives to the voice and presence of Jesus.

As I sat with my eyes closed, I saw something like flashes of lightning and I saw countless instances from years before in my life where I was being tempted by things that were actually looking for me. Image after image and scene after scene was being played back before my very eyes. They were countless times from earlier in my life and all the way up through my teenage years where I was being faced with overwhelming temptations.

After a few seconds, which in the moment felt like a lifetime, I heard the voice of the Holy Spirit again. This time He brought words to my heart that caused me to break down. I heard the Holy Spirit say to me,

"Your children, and children's children, will not have to contend with the same forces that you have battled your entire life." You may not realize the magnitude of the moment that was happening there for me, so let me explain.

I believe that fasting has the power to break generational curses. If you do not believe in generational curses, I am sorry, and pray that the Lord would bring revelation to your life on these matters. I believe in generational curses because I have contended with them and have been set free from them by the hand of the Lord and the power of the Spirit. In one moment the Lord can bring clarity into your life to things that have always been misunderstood.

In one moment the Lord can bring clarity into your life to things that have always been misunderstood.

In just a moment, or with a simple word, God can give you a totally new perspective or understanding into situations you thought you previously had figured out or weren't even paying attention to. Situations over the course of your life that you didn't even realize had a different explanation than what you had experienced up until that moment can all be thoroughly explained to you with just one word from God. This is amazing! This was the case for me. In a moment I gained understanding about things in my life that have since changed me.

Looking at my family tree I saw my parents, grandparents, and other relatives, and I began to notice patterns. There were threads that ran through years and generations. To the natural thinker, and by that I mean someone without the mind of the Holy Spirit, this might seem like harmless and natural. It might seem like simple biological traits carried through generations by DNA. But by looking at either side, my mother's or father's, I began to recognize certain themes. To use a more biblical term, I saw generations of strongholds.

On one side of the family, alcoholism and addiction run throughout the lives of people as far back as I know. On another side adulterous living and promiscuity had their run throughout. Looking back, it would have been amazing if someone would have sat me down when I was a younger man and said to me, "Mike, I need you to understand some things. I want to tell you about certain strongholds, or generational curses, that have ravaged our family line for years because I do not want you to be ignorant about what is working against you. There are forces working against you that desire to have complete control of your life." You have no idea how great of a talk that would have been for me. It never happened.

As a younger man I was not able to grasp why I had such an overwhelming struggle with certain temptations. I didn't understand why things like alcohol or experimentation with sexual behavior were so appealing to me. I couldn't figure out why I constantly found myself battling with desires and strong cravings for things that I didn't even really know about. Of course, culture, our environment, and even biological factors create space for this. But the enemy spends generations tormenting our families and uses all of these as avenues where he can gain leverage over us and our seed.

You see, had I been set up with the talk that we just mentioned, I would have had a fighting chance and been alerted to the size of the battle. At least I would have understood that for whatever reason, people in my family line seemed to have struggles in certain areas. It would not have caught me by surprise. When these issues came knocking on my door I would have been prepared to respond. Instead, I was overwhelmed in any attempts to resist the things working against me.

I am not trying to make excuses here for my behavior. I am telling you that someone who is living outside of God's voice and presence in their life does not have a chance against spiritual and generational enemies. My family was not walking with the Lord, nor was there any knowledge of God or life of Christ installed into my heart when I was young.

Without God, even the strongest individual can be worn down. Over time all of us can be overcome. You may be able to resist the initial attraction. You may do well to abstain from a few seductive invitations. But when the onslaught continues against you and the only power source you have to draw from is yourself, you are not in a fair fight. The deck is stacked against any person who cannot see into the spiritual realm. This is where I found myself. It's where many Christians remain long after getting "saved."

> **Without God, even the strongest individual can be worn down. Over time all of us can be overcome.**

Under the circumstances, I caved in to the temptations and did a really good job of ruining my life. It all started by me not being willing to fight. After a while, the things coming against me led me to think that something was wrong with me. I began to think that the things that came against me were a part of who I was. I took ownership of my struggles, as if they were being initiated from within me. I did not know how to tell the difference. In fact, I did not even know there was a difference.

When I came into agreement with what was working against me I lost the fight altogether. There is power in agreement. It was when Eve chose to agree with what the devil was saying to her in the garden and move out of agreement with what God had already said that she and Adam found themselves in trouble. As a matter of fact, it was because they came into agreement with the devil that they lost dominion over ground that God had already given to them.

When we are not aware that there is a spiritual battle taking place over the control of our lives, we easily fall prey to the devices and tactics of the enemy of our souls. The devil and all the forces of hell would love nothing more than for you to ignore them, believe they do not really exist, and consider all of this type of talk to be foolish. There is a point in the Scriptures that I believe illustrates our point and can help to provide some greater insight.

In Mark chapter 5 we read of a situation where Jesus encounters another man that has been demonized for quite some time. I think it would be best for you to see the account straight from Mark's writing. Let's pick it up with verse 1,

> "Then they came to the other side of the sea, to the region of the Gerasenes. As soon as He got out of the boat, a man with an unclean spirit came out of the tombs and met Him. He lived in the tombs. No one was able to restrain him anymore—even with chains—because he often

had been bound with shackles and chains, but had snapped off the chains and smashed the shackles. No one was strong enough to subdue him. And always, night and day, he was crying out among the tombs and in the mountains and cutting himself with stones."[46]

Before we dive into the story, let's make sure we are on the same page. I don't know if you have ever encountered anyone in your life that has been demonized. Another way to describe the man's condition is to call him demon possessed. I have encountered such situations, and I can tell you that it is no joke. When you witness a situation such as the one that is being described by Mark, the last thing on your mind is deciding if it's real or not. There are real demonic forces and influences from hell that are not simply looking to become your friend; they want to take control of and destroy your entire life. Such was the case for the man that we have just read about approaching Jesus. Let's get back to our story with verse 6,

> "When he saw Jesus from a distance, he ran and knelt down before Him. He cried out with a loud voice, 'What do You have to do with me,

---
[46] Mark 5:1-5, HCSB

Jesus, Son of the Most High God? I beg You before God, don't torment me!' For He had told him, 'Come out of the man, you unclean spirit! What is your name?' He asked him. 'My name is Legion,' he answered Him, 'because we are many.' *And he kept begging Him not to send them out of the region.*"[47]

For those of you who are familiar with this passage you know that Jesus ends up casting the legion out and sending them into a nearby herd of pigs. Upon entering the pigs, the demons head straight down a steep bank and plunge into the sea to drown. This didn't sit well with the owner of the pigs. His business was now sinking before his eyes. You could say Jesus ruined this guy's livelihood.

There is something very interesting about this interaction between Jesus and the legion of demons. It points to a specific bondage over the man. Of all the things that the demons could have asked Jesus for, their request seems to be very specific. I want to draw your attention to it again. The request of the legion to Jesus was this, "Let us stay in this region." The legion realized that it was no match for the Son of God. The legion also realized that it was okay to come out of

---

[47] Mark 5:6-10, HCSB (emphasis added)

the man, as long as it was permitted to remain in the region. Stay in the region? Why would this be their one request? How does the region relate to the demonic forces currently possessing this man? I would like to try and provide an answer.

There are high places in spiritual wickedness and darkness. The word uses these very terms many times. We have to understand and gain some context for the passage above by seeing what Paul speaks about in Ephesians when he says these words, "For we wrestle not against flesh and blood, but against principalities, against powers, against the rulers of the darkness of this world, against spiritual wickedness in high places."[48] Daniel chapter 10 also speaks of conflict in the higher places that held a heavenly messenger from being released to Daniel.[49] We need to see that this is not just some biblical allegory, but that it is very real.

Let me replace a word that's found at the end of the biblical interaction between Jesus and legion. Let's take the word region and replace it with the word household. It would read much different if it said, "And he kept begging Him not to send them out of the household." That kind of changes the tone a little, doesn't it? Let's take the word household out

---

[48] Eph. 6:12, KJV
[49] Dan. 10:13

and replace it with whatever your last name is. What if the verse that we just came across were to read this way, "And they kept begging Him not to send them out of the _____ family"? You may think that this seems a little silly, but I pray that you see this subject a little differently than you did just a few minutes ago. There is a severity to the implications of what we are discussing right now.

Many times we just pass situations off as the status quo, or "normal life." Many times when we feel we are up against things that we do not really have control over we come up with a way to excuse it. Have you ever looked at anyone in your family and found yourself saying these words, "Oh, he is just like so-and-so"? Or, "You know, she is just like her mama." "The reason he is like that is because his grandfather was like that." All of these seemingly harmless comments have a way of shedding light onto what we are talking about right now.

What if I told you that you did not have to simply just think that addiction was always going to be a part of your family's story? What if you knew there was a way for your family to be free from alcoholism? What if someone sat you down and told you that although up until now everyone in your family line has always dealt with abusive behavior and fits of rage, it did not have to continue being that way? Would you want to know how? Would you want the pathway to this freedom? I believe you would. Anyone would.

Fasting and prayer has the power to break the hold of demonic strongholds that linger over your life. Fasting and prayer has the ability to sever the ties of oppression from the enemy that has been attached to your life. I believe with all of my heart that you, just like me, can be set free and be the one to repair the breach in your own life and lineage.

It is important that you understand I am not saying God cannot deal with any issue in one powerful moment of deliverance. Actually, in the moment of turning to the salvation of the Gospel all of these things are dealt with by Christ's finished work of the cross. But for different reasons, different people do not immediately and completely experience the reality of that freedom. Although we have the right to freedom, and these bondages have no more eternal claim over us, for many of us God's ordained pathway to freedom is found in the process of walking it out. If you have already come to Christ and see some of these battles continuing in your life or family line, fasting might just be the very way to engage the Lord and walk with Him in breaking generational bondages over your life and lineage.

You don't have to surrender to demonic assignments that have been sent to hover over your family line. You don't have to lay down and die in regard to these issues, struggles, and weapons that have been formed against your family and personal life. You don't need to think that you will always be a certain way or that it is simply just how people in your family line have always had to struggle. There is power when we throw our lives into fasting and prayer! There is power, not because of our piety or our own goodness, but because Jesus is with us and for us!

Principalities

There are realities in this world that will only be confronted by a man or woman who is willing to continually give themselves to a lifestyle of fasting and prayer. There are strongholds, principalities, and governing forces of darkness that will only be contended with by a man or woman who has postured themselves before God in fasting. Anyone who has given their life over to God in the continued place of fasting has become a deadly weapon against rulers and authorities of dark places.

I want to be very transparent with you about my situation in hopes that you will find a pathway to Jesus. I pray that He will bring you freedom in the areas we have been discussing. When I got saved, when Jesus found me and rescued me from myself and the power of sin and death, it was glorious. I was instantly a radically different person. My desires changed. Everything about me seemed to be made new. However, as deep as this was, there was still something that seemed to linger in my life. I would have a tough day at the office and be walking through the grocery store at the end of the day and a voice would whisper to me, "Mike, it's okay if you just have one...." Usually during stressful times a voice from out of nowhere would catch my attention with words like these, "You know, there's nothing wrong with you grabbing just one drink. Mike, really, it is allowed in the Scriptures...." This happened pretty regularly for me.

> **Anyone who has given their life over to God in the continued place of fasting has become a deadly weapon against rulers and authorities of dark places.**

It is important to explain that I was in love with Jesus. I was walking with Jesus for several years while all of this continued. I was working full time and also serving in several different capacities in my local church. I am not talking about a struggle that I had two weeks into salvation. What I am explaining to you here is something that was an ongoing process for me. It was something that really needed to be confronted. I just didn't know how to confront it or what it could be confronted by.

Simultaneously, at the time my wife and I married everything was pretty great. Sure, we were working through your typical newlywed situations and learning to live with one another, but overall life was relatively easy. There would be times where we would have disagreements, like any normal couple. It was during these moments, many not even all that stressful, a voice would whisper to me, "Mike, you don't have to take this...there's someone else out there that will treat you the way you deserve to be treated." Or, I might hear something like, "You don't have to stay married to her. Things are never going to get any better...they will only get worse. Get out while you still have a chance."

There is a place of union with Christ by which He is able to rise within us and crush the work of the enemy against us.

Can you see what is happening here? I was in a place where I had been saved. I was set free from a past life of sin and addiction, and I genuinely loved Jesus. Yet, with all of this going right, I was still having to contend with the voices. Those voices, though they didn't have control over me, were continuing to come against me.

I am not saying that once you come to Christ you are never going to experience temptation anymore.

That would be foolish and unbiblical expectations. We will always be tempted. There will always be your old life that wants you back. The devil hates the image of Jesus in you and will stop at nothing to steal, kill, and destroy those who belong to Jesus. What I am saying is that we don't have to be those who are continually overwhelmed by the pressures and forces working against us. There is a place of union with Christ by which He is able to rise within us and crush the work of the enemy against us. There is a place of beautiful and experiential union with Jesus that frees us from the pressure of trying to work things out in our own strength.

I love Jesus. I am happily married. I am now years into walking with the Lord and experiencing the freedom that comes to those who walk in the Holy Spirit. I am also still contending with assignments that have hovered over my family line from before my birth. But things drastically changed when Jesus asked me to meet Him in the place of a forty-day fast. At the end of the forty days, when I heard the words, "You have repaired the breach," I didn't realize the significance in that moment. I wasn't able to fully grasp the weight of what was being communicated to me. But I would love to testify to you that from that moment I have been a changed man! From that moment nothing has been the same.

Sure the voices may attempt to return. Sure the enemy attempts to make that just another situation where you have some spiritual excitement for a little while and then always return to being the same person. This was not that and I have never looked back. From that moment there has been a new place of freedom. This freedom has impacted my entire life and provided rest in the Lord that you just cannot fake. I believe that through the place of fasting the Lord was able to raise up a standard against that which had haunted my life, continually waiting for moments to take advantage of me.

> **My obedience brought me into breakthrough I was not discerning enough to pray for.**

Just like the man who came to Jesus while his life was being ravaged by the work of the enemy, you also can be freed. You too can experience the same power that Jesus had when He spoke and released that man from the forces of hell that were assigned to him for generations. I am absolutely sure there is another way Jesus could set you free. However, I am sharing my experience of deliverance through responding in obedience to the invitation of fasting.

You need to understand that I never asked for God to do this in my life. I did not even realize something needed to be done. This was not the hot item sitting at the top of my prayer list for weeks on end when God decided that He would step in and intervene on my behalf. It actually didn't look anything like that. I was walking with Jesus in obedience to an invitation given to me. At the time it seemed like an isolated invitation, which just happened to be a forty-day fast. It was not until the end of that long and faithful road that the Holy Spirit spoke to me. He said something that I was not ready for. It was unexpected, and it was initiated by God. My obedience brought me into breakthrough I was not discerning enough to pray for.

I believe when the Word says that God is no respecter of persons.[50] I believe that He is the same yesterday, today, and forever.[51] I believe that the examples for us in the Scriptures are not isolated events recorded so we can idolize the men and women we find there. Rather, the stories we find in His Word are there to provoke us and reveal the invitation being offered to us. The stories of how God has met and walked with people over the history of recorded time should cause our eyes to be opened to the personal invitations of encounter found within their story.

There are generational curses waiting to be broken and defeated. There are principalities hovering over cities, regions, and nations that God is waiting to use

---

[50] Rom. 2:11
[51] Heb. 13:8

someone to tear down. Fasting is a critical medium by which God has determined to assault many of these high places. Give your life to the assault. Give your life to Jesus and the lifestyle of fasting.

8

Types

I would like to now turn a corner and consider some different types of biblical fasts. If we can change the question from "if" I will fast to "when," it will be beneficial to have an understanding of the various fasts we might participate in. Some may be led by spiritual hunger, while others may be invited in by the Holy Spirit's calling. If we are living by the Voice, the Lord will speak to you about stepping into fasting and prayer with Him. Most people wrestle with questions of how to enter a fast. Do you just schedule times of fasting over the course of the year, or do you wait for the Lord to lead you into every fast that you do? This is a great question. My answer to this is: Yes, and, yes.

I am convinced that it is greatly beneficial to have times during the year that you know you will be fasting;

disciplined scheduling that will keep you in the life rhythm of fasting. But I am also absolutely committed to following the voice of the Lord day by day. Being sensitive enough to whatever I may feel that day or moment the Holy Spirit is saying is how I experience spontaneity in fasting.

There will be times that you wake up in the morning and the Holy Spirit will say to you, "Why don't you skip breakfast this morning and be with Me?" It is then up to you on whether or not you are going to yield your life to the spontaneous prompting. This is just an example of what I mean by the spontaneous leading of the Lord. It could be something that was not in your plans and doesn't really go along with what is comfortable for you or anything you have ever done before.

One of the greatest joys of this life is continually cultivating a "yes" on the inside, within your heart, to the leading of the Lord as you walk with Him! We will return and talk more about this at the end of the chapter. For now, we'll take a look at a few different types of ways we can approach fasting. We will start with Daniel, and what has become known as the Daniel fast.

Daniel

The first type of fast that we will take a look at will be what is commonly referred to as a "Daniel fast." The reason that we call it a Daniel fast is because it stems from the fast that the prophet Daniel used. Daniel was a man that walked with God regularly in fasting and prayer. In Daniel's life there are some precious things that we are able to glean from specifically on the subject of fasting.

Daniel was a young prophet that was taken into captivity in Babylon. Though in captivity in a foreign land, Daniel committed himself to the Lord and continued to walk with Him faithfully in that place. In chapter 1 of the book of Daniel we find that the king of Babylon is looking to recruit some of the young men that had been taken into captivity into his service. He sends Ashpenaz, the chief of his court officials, to begin the search for some Israelites from the royal family and the nobility—young men without any physical defect, handsome, showing aptitude for every kind of learning, well informed, quick to understand, and qualified to teach in the king's palace.[52]

Daniel is included in those young men who are taken into training along with three of his Hebrew friends, Shadrach, Meshach, and Abednego. The king assigned them a daily amount of food and wine from his very own table. They were to be trained for a period of three years, and after that they were to enter into the king's service.[53] Although this may seem like

---

[52] Dan. 1:3-4, NIV
[53] Dan. 1:5, NIV

a pretty great job for a slave, Daniel made a decision and led some of his friends to take a unique stand of purity. Daniel said they would not defile themselves with royal food and wine, and he gained permission for his diet from the chief official. Though the official was afraid they might be malnourished and therefore be less fit for the king's service, God granted favor, and the official granted Daniel's request.

Scripture says Daniel asked the official, "Please test your servants *for ten days: Give us nothing but vegetables to eat and water to drink*. Then compare our appearance with that of the young men who eat the royal food, and treat your servants in accordance with what you see."[54] At the end of the ten days Daniel and his three friends looked healthier and better nourished than any of the young men who ate the royal food.

This is at the very least counterintuitive. Let's first begin by saying that if there was ever a time that you felt you were in a place where you could not fast, Daniel and his friends had found it. I say that because there will always be reasons why you should not fast. There will always be a birthday party, a work gathering, a holiday with tons of food, or some other reason sharing a meal with people is more important than sharing the Bread of Life. If you are one that is

---

[54] Dan. 1:12-13, NIV (emphasis added)

constantly looking for a reason not to fast, you won't have to look far. Daniel and his friends did not give in to the thought, "This is not a good time to start fasting," even though they were being evaluated for a life-or-death job. These radical young men simply went for it and obeyed God.

Maybe you are asking the same question that I asked myself when considering this account. Where in the world did Daniel get the idea to eat just vegetables and drink nothing but water for ten days? I believe we find our answer in verse 8, "But Daniel resolved not to defile himself...." Daniel was a man who was committed to walking with God. I believe that in this place of resolve, God spoke to Daniel and gave him the blueprint for how he would not defile himself.

Maybe the Holy Spirit helped Daniel to see that being attached to the luxuries of royal life would cloud his mind from hearing the voice of God. I believe this because of the way that God responded to their fasting. Verse 17 tells us that to these four young men God gave knowledge and understanding of all kinds of literature and learning. God gave Daniel the ability to understand dreams and visions of all kinds. Wow! This is an incredible response to their decision to walk with God in this way of fasting.

There is another place in Daniel's life that he is found fasting that the Scriptures record, and it is found in chapter 10. And similar to the account above, God seemed to lead Daniel in a very specific manner, even outlining which things would be fit for him to eat according to how God wanted to speak to him. At the end of chapter 9 Daniel is praying and repenting on behalf of the people. Daniel records that,

> "Then the man Gabriel, whom I had seen in the vision previously, came to me in my extreme weariness about the time of the evening offering. He gave me instruction and talked with me and said, "O Daniel, I have now come forth to give you insight with understanding. At the beginning of your supplications the command was issued, and I have come to tell you, for you are highly esteemed; so give heed to the message and gain understanding of the vision."[55]

Daniel is quite possibly one of the most revelatory individuals you will find in the Old Testament. Daniel is having full-blown visions, dreams, angelic encounters, and experiences that are pretty amazing. Daniel is interpreting dreams for others, and is even telling others what they dreamed and then telling them why, as was the case with King Nebuchadnezzar.[56]

---

[55] Dan. 9:21-23
[56] Dan. 2:17-38

It is right after this encounter with Gabriel, at the end of Daniel chapter 9, that we find the record that he was fasting. Chapter 10 begins with Daniel being terrified by the vision that has been revealed to him. It is at this point that verse 2 tells us, "In those days *I Daniel was mourning three full weeks. I ate no pleasant bread, neither came flesh nor wine in my mouth,* nor did I anoint myself at all, till three whole weeks were fulfilled."[57] From this place Daniel is taken into another glorious encounter where it is revealed to him that, "From the first day you purposed to understand and to humble yourself before your God, your prayers were heard. I have come because of your prayers. But the prince of the kingdom of Persia opposed me for twenty-one days. Then Michael, one of the chief princes, came to help me after I had been left there with the kings of Persia. Now I have come to help you understand...."[58]

I think it is evident that Daniel was a man that was committed to walking with God. And because of his resolve to walk with God, Daniel's life broke into some extraordinary experiences. We can now look more closely at the two different instances of Daniel's fasting. In chapter 1 we saw that Daniel and his friends determined that for ten days they would eat only vegetables and drink nothing but water. Then in chapter

---

[57] Dan. 10:2-3, KJV (emphasis added)
[58] Dan. 10:12-14, HCSB

10 we find that Daniel is alone fasting for three full weeks, or twenty-one days, and he is not eating bread, or meat, or drinking wine. These are the two Daniel fasts that we find in the life of Daniel.

Daniel fasts have actually become sort of fashionable in our day. There are a lot of modifications that have been made to Daniel's original fast. There are plenty of great resources and websites out where you can look further into "foods allowed." Although we do this to gain a better understanding of how to posture ourselves during this type of fast, what is of greatest importance is that you allow the Lord to determine the blueprint for you and that you commit to walking in that place.

As you can see, the first time we biblically see a Daniel fast, or Daniel fasting, it is nothing but vegetables to eat and water to drink. However, later when Daniel is found fasting again it is this time no bread, no meat, and no wine. Both are Daniel fasts, yet both are not the same. It is important that you really listen for the Lord to lay out to you what is being expected of you during the plan for this fast.

I find it interesting that when Daniel knew he was going to fast again in chapter 10 that he did not just rely upon the same old method to produce a certain result. Daniel didn't just fast again for ten days the same exact way as before because it was what God said last time. Daniel looked to the Lord in a fresh way and waited for God to once again lay out the terms of his next fast. This is key to how we approach the Lord in fasting.

It is easy to try to corner the moving of the Holy Spirit in your life with formulas, processes, and systems. It would have been easy for Daniel to say, "Well, you know last time we received some pretty incredible things from God by fasting this way…let's just do that again." But this is not what Daniel did, and neither should we. We cannot just systemize our walk with God. Daniel leaned upon the voice of God to speak to him day by day, and to lead him day by day, and because of that chosen posture God was faithful.

We cannot just systemize our walk with God.

Take a moment to consider what I am about to say to you. Daniel didn't have a system; he had a voice. Daniel didn't live by a system or a magic formula in his life. He walked with God and gave himself to whatever he heard the Lord saying to him in the moment. Daniel did not just have godly mechanics to rely upon; he had the voice of the living God. Daniel lived a life that was led. There have been times for me that the Lord has said, "Okay, this time we are going strictly vegetables and water." And there have been other times where it has just been the removal of meat. It is important that we keep an ear to hear so that we can posture ourselves correctly.

Fasting is a key way that we continually see the Lord preparing Daniel for the different seasons he entered in life. Fasting is one of the channels that God used to speak to Daniel in interpreting the wild experiences He ordained for his life. Because of the fasting and prayer, which Daniel would not compromise on, God was able to use him as a clear mouthpiece across the reign of at least six different kings and their kingdoms. Fasting, without a doubt, was an invaluable practice in Daniel's life.

Daniel didn't have a system; he had a voice.

We see that all of the young men were given wisdom and understanding. However, to Daniel was also given the ability to interpret dreams and visions of all kinds. Also, on numerous occasions angelic messengers come to Daniel to give him insight and understanding to the visions and experiences that he and others were having. There are multiple encounters with angelic messengers for very specific purposes recorded in Daniel's life. Please take note; this was not just for spiritual enjoyment and cool stories to talk about. Each encounter had a design from heaven leading into fulfilling God's purposes.

Absolute

Another type of fast that we will look at is an absolute fast. When we talk about an absolute fast, what we are actually saying is that we are not going to eat any food or drink, anything at all. In order to get a better understanding of an absolute fast we will look to the book of Esther. It is this "absolute" style of fasting that is mentioned in Esther as she rallies the Jewish people to a time of consecration before she enters into the presence of the king. Esther tells the people, "Go, gather together all the Jews who are in Susa, and fast for me. Do not eat or drink for three days, night or day. I and my maidens also will fast in the same way. And thus I will go in to the king, which is not according to the law; and if I perish, I perish."[59] Esther called the people to three days of absolutely no eating or drinking.

It is also believed by many that Elijah's forty-day fast was one to be of this "absolute" nature as well.[60] But this is extremely abnormal—even supernatural—and not recommended outside of hearing specifically from the Lord and being accountable to others both spiritually and medically. Again, the prime importance is on obeying the voice of the Lord, but in this case it

---
[59] Est. 4:16
[60] 1 Kings 19:8

is important to use both wisdom and humility when approaching an absolute fast.

Liquid Fast

In Luke chapter 4 and verse 1 we find, "Then Jesus returned from the Jordan, full of the Holy Spirit, and was led by the Spirit in the wilderness for forty days to be tempted by the Devil. *He ate nothing during those days*, and when they were over, He was hungry."[61] Just as Jesus was found to be in the wilderness for a period of forty days, and as He ate nothing during those days, this is what we mean by a liquid fast. Jesus fasted for forty days, though a liquid fast can be whatever time frame the Lord may speak to you about.

There are different variations of a liquid fast. A liquid fast can mean nothing but water. It can also mean just liquids: water, fruit juice, clear broth, etc. The parameters are pretty straightforward; just don't eat anything. During this fast you'd consume no solids, not even blended! With this type of fast there have been all types of modifications and adjustments made for various reasons. What is important is to note the words found in verse 1 that we just read, "Then Jesus was led by the Spirit...." Being led by the Spirit in your

---

[61] Luke 4:1-2, HCSB

life is what we are highlighting. The Spirit will lead you personally into what He is looking for you to do.

What is special here is the contrast in Jesus' condition as He enters into the wilderness before the time of fasting, compared to the way that He exits the wilderness. Verse 14 of Luke chapter 4 tells us, "Then Jesus returned to Galilee in the power of the Spirit...."[62] Jesus goes in full of the Spirit and comes out full of the power of the Spirit. Jesus immediately comes out of the wilderness after having been tested and overcoming the devil himself.

> **The Spirit will lead you personally into what He is looking for you to do.**

After this experience there is a notable difference in the life of Christ. Jesus is now marked by powerful declaration and demonstration of signs, wonders, and miracles. We see this in the events that take place immediately upon His return to Galilee. Jesus is teaching the people on the Sabbath and Scripture says they were amazed at His teaching and the authority of His message. In the synagogue there was a man possessed by the spirit of an unclean demon, and Jesus delivered the man and drove the demon out. The people's reaction is provided to us in saying, "And amazement

---

[62] Luke 4:14, HCSB

came upon them all, and they began talking with one another saying, 'What is this message? For with authority and power He commands the unclean spirits and they come out.'"[63]

Jesus' obedience to His Father in the place of fasting seems to have brought a remarkable change upon His life. It is beautiful to see Jesus obeying the Father in fasting. It is encouraging to see the Son of God laying out a clear example of what it means to give our lives over to the leading of the Spirit. Searching for the power is something that many will consume themselves with. However, whether that is your outcome isn't yours to decide. But the giving of yourself in obedience to the leading of the Spirit is something you can decide right now. It is a sign of maturity and real trust to keep your heart centered on cultivating a yes to the leading of the Spirit and leaving the results up to the Father.

Sunup to Sundown

This is a fasting style that many have found to be easier to begin with if you do not have a history with fasting. This is a fast that includes, just as the name reveals, fasting from sunup to sundown over the course of a day or many days. Traditionally this would

---

[63] Luke 4:31-36

be a liquid fast, but you could very well also choose to do a sunup to sundown Daniel fast, or be led to a juice fast or the fasting of a particular food item over the course of a day until sundown.

It is also important to understand that by sunup to sundown, what is really being implied here is that you are only going to eat dinner every day. The goal is not to wake up before the sun rises and gorge yourself so that you can make it on a full belly all day until the sun goes down, when you can do it again. This would completely defeat the purpose of fasting this way. What I have found as I have been invited into fasting this way has been very special, even life changing. Sunup to sundown fasting brings us into a place of great surrender on a daily basis. Daily I am committing to the Lord to refrain from certain things. Daily I am surrendering the strength of my will.

Sunup to sundown fasting is obviously much different than liquid fasting. But what I mean is this: A sunup to sundown fast has the feeling of day one every day. To those who have ever done a liquid fast before, I am sure you are very aware of that day-one feeling. Every day is like the first day all over again. You never get to the place of "extended" fasting where your hunger pains dissolve and you are able to maintain the "sweet spot." By "sweet spot" I mean the place in a fast where your hunger pains diminish and no longer seem to overwhelm you to the point of dominating your focus.

Keep in mind we are not fasting to prove to God or ourselves how mighty we are. We are not fasting in order to reveal to those around us how religious we can be. We definitely are not fasting so that our lives can become visible and we can be held in high regard because of our effort. In fact, we should be seeking the opposite—humility, quietness of spirit, and personal encounter with Jesus—during fasting.

> **There is no effective substitute for having the voice of God in your life.**

Sunup to sundown fasting deals directly with that surrendering of the will. The surrendering of our will on a daily basis in an intensified way is something that God will use in order to bring you into greater places of submission. This submission is needed at times in order for Him to lead you more clearly. The daily softening of your heart and determination to relinquish your control over to God has a profound effect on those who take up sunup to sundown fasting. There have been significant times in my life where sunup to sundown fasting played a major role when the Lord wanted to lead me in very specific ways. The surrendering of your will and relinquishing your control are necessities to walking with Jesus and truly being led by Him. Sunup to sundown fasting has a special way of fine-tuning your submission to where you can be led day by day.

Ezekiel's Posture

I don't think we can spend enough time trying to drive home the importance of living a life that is truly led by the voice of the Lord. There is no effective substitute for having the voice of God in your life. Jesus said, "My sheep listen to My voice; I know them, and they follow Me."[64] He desires to speak to you. He desires to guide you. He wants to be the One to navigate you through life's pathways. He will do it, if you wait for Him and allow Him to.

Ezekiel is another prophet that I want to look at. Ezekiel is taken up by the hand of the Lord in an encounter and brought to a valley of dry bones. While there, the Lord asks Ezekiel the question, "Ezekiel, can these bones live?" I love Ezekiel's response and wholeheartedly believe that it is just what we need to consider as we give ourselves to a lifestyle of fasting and prayer. Ezekiel says back to the Lord, "Oh Lord, you alone know...."[65]

Ezekiel's response to God's question should be our desired posture in fasting and prayer. Actually, our

---

[64] John 10:27, NIV
[65] Eze. 37:1-3, NLT

goal should be to find Ezekiel's posture in every facet of our life. *You alone know* is the ultimate way to keep our lives rightly postured before God. *You alone know* indicates the surrender of our wisdom and ability to reason out everything in our life. *You alone know* reveals the fact that we don't really know. *You alone know* is not just remaining in a place where we realize that we don't have all of the answers or the ultimate wisdom in any given situation, but it is confirming that God really is the only One who does.

As we wait upon the Lord in fasting and prayer we should keep Ezekiel's answer close to our heart. Realizing that God alone is the One who knows exactly what we need in every season of our life and in every situation that we will face should provide us with a great amount of freedom to obey Him and walk in step with the Spirit. Understanding that God is in control should free us from the manipulative control that we attempt to exert on our situations, and even on God Himself, with certain types of behavior.

With all we have discussed regarding the different types of fasts, I believe that it is important that we keep something in mind. In all of the biblical fasts that we have seen thus far, the people we have read about did not know what outcome awaited them at the close of their fasts. These people were simply walking with God in the way that they felt the moment required.

We see the outcome and then assume it as we read of the beginning of their obedience. But for them this was not the case. They never saw it coming. These men were simply walking with God and believing that whatever it was that God was asking them to do was sufficient to keep them in sync with the work of the Spirit in their life.

Again, we are not fasting in order to get wisdom, power, or anything else for that matter. If we are not careful we can very easily find ourselves in a place where we are fasting with the goal of achieving any of a slew of different things. We can easily be motivated to fast and pray so that God would do something or give us something, and this is simply not the way that it should be. This is manipulative of our relationship with Him. This kind of thinking opens a door for a twisted perspective; the kind that thinks we can control God by certain behaviors or activities. Our life is to be one that is beautifully led and sculpted by God, and that being in the specially designed way that He knows we need shaping in specific seasons.

By surveying your life right now, how would you know what it is that you truly needed? You wouldn't if you were honest. The best that you and I are able to do is to guess and hope for the best. We have no idea of what tomorrow will bring, and for that reason even our best plans are subject to change far beyond our control. But in all of our lack of knowing, God knows! And this is one of the foundational reasons that we give our lives to obedience.

Obedience to the Lord, specifically in the area of fasting and prayer, will always equip you for whatever it is that life may be walking you through. Herein lies the heart of the matter: **You will never be all that God knows you can be without fasting and prayer.** You see, we are beings partially made of flesh and led by the sensual functions of our bodies. Fasting directly targets that physical part of us which needs to be submitted to the Spirit of God in order that His Spirit in us can have His place as the Master of our lives.

Rather than attempting to control your situations, it is far more effective to respond to God and let Him do what He knows He needs to do. This should be our cry in every season of life, *Oh Lord, You alone know!* I don't really know what I need. I don't have a clear enough understanding of what is out in front of me or the way that things need to end up, but God, You do. God, You know what is best for me. God, You know all that I will need in this next season for the things that I am going to end up facing that I don't even realize are there right now. So I will press into You. I will forego the voices and needs of my flesh and position myself to better hear Your voice. I will live a fasted life of dedication to You. And I will follow however You may lead me in this place!

9

Practical

As we discuss some of the practical things that you will experience as you fast, weight loss is not going to be part of the discussion. If you would like to fast—regularly, intermittently, or extended—in order to shed weight, there are materials and resources that you can look to elsewhere for more information. However, there are some amazing benefits and some intense struggles that you will experience when you fast. It is important to be prepared for the things that will happen to our bodies. This is not going to be a comprehensive list, but rather a highlight of some key points to be aware of as we venture out into fasting.

Also, if you have health conditions that prevent you from fasting, it is important to exercise wisdom in these areas. If there are reasons now that have you regularly seeing a doctor, you should be asking questions about how to approach fasting in your specific situation. However, it is important to divide between the fear of the unknown, so commonly presented as wisdom, and real medical concerns that would keep you from stepping into what the Lord is calling you to.

Let me say this again to make sure that it can be as clear as possible: I do not claim to be a doctor. I do not want this to seem to be an all-inclusive text on fasting. Please execute wisdom in these matters as you walk with the Lord, being led by the Spirit. I want you to be successful in fasting, and that requires you being aware of your own personal context. Begin as slowly as you need to begin. We are all leaning in toward the same conclusion, which is an encounter with Christ, even if our starting points seem to be somewhat different. Listen for the Lord's leading. He really is a good father in this way. Begin wherever you have to and just start faithfully running. If it be one day, two days, a single meal at first, do whatever you must; just begin.

Detoxing

There are incredible health benefits to fasting. Up until this point we have covered the spiritual aspect of fasting, which is rightfully the most important part of a fast intended to draw us near to Jesus. However, there are some amazing things that your body will benefit from while fasting. We will look at several benefits, the first of which is detoxing. Detoxing can be defined as treatment designed to rid the body of poisonous substances. Detoxification is a normal body process of eliminating or neutralizing the toxins resulting from biochemical functions through the colon, liver, kidneys, lungs, lymph nodes, and skin. Fasting precipitates this process because when food no longer enters the body, the body turns to its fat reserves for energy.[66] When the fat reserves are used for energy during a fast, they release the stored toxic chemicals from the fatty acids into the system, which are then eliminated through the above-mentioned organs.

Though this sounds great, I must mention some of the challenges that can arise during a period of detoxification. You are probably familiar with the term detox being applied to alcohol and substance addiction. Just like with those addictions, when your body has built up a dependence on something and you decide to sever the ties, there are going to be some battles to fight. Some of the things that you can experience while fasting are due to the body detoxing and eliminating toxins. Irritability, mood swings, fatigue, headaches (mild or severe), increased hunger pains, cravings, cramping, a film over your tongue, bad breath, and even blurred

---

[66] "Fasting For Detox," *Pure Inside Out*, http://www.pureinsideout.com/fasting-for-detox.html.

vision are all some examples. This is a normal result of the body not getting the food it is expecting.

To compound these effects, if you are consuming caffeine on a daily basis, whether it be one or multiple cups of coffee, energy drinks, or workout supplements, removing caffeine will cause your body to experience a certain level of shock. For however long the time period has been that you have been faithfully providing your body with caffeine, once removed cold turkey, there will be anywhere from a mild to severe battle to get through. Certain things like this should be considered in your approach to a fast. The more dependencies you can wean off and the "cleaner" your diet is when you begin your fast, the less intense the physical and mental detox will be.

When planning to begin a fast it will be important to get started the right way. Try not to overeat leading into the beginning of your time of fasting. Minimize your portion sizes when you know that you will be entering into a fast in the next day or two to avoid the overwhelming hunger at the onset of the fast. Make sure to increase your water intake in the days leading into the beginning of your fast as well.

Why do I take the time to mention such things? I am glad you asked. I want to make the process really simple and clear. I don't want you to be caught off guard by the natural progressions of fasting. Your thing may not be caffeine. That's okay, because the principle can be applied to a wide variety of things like soda, candy, alcohol, or certain types of food. Things that create emotional satisfaction, rushes, or highs are all going to be harder to break free from. I mention this in order for you to be sober and alert to what you are going to potentially walk through when you commit to fasting with the Lord.

I hope that this knowledge can prepare you to tackle the potential excuses that might have kept you from fulfilling an invitation by the Spirit to fast. I hope that when you begin fasting and you all of a sudden get a bad headache, you don't feel like you are about to die because you are doing something wrong. The headache is not your sign of confirmation that you need to stop dead in your tracks and turn back to the refrigerator. The headache can be an indicator that your body has been dependent on something that it is now detoxing from.

If you suddenly end up with blurred vision, which I have gone through countless times, I hope that you do not automatically think that your time of fasting is dangerous and allow the enemy to talk you out of continuing for the sake of some discomfort. Now, I am not talking about blurred vision that stems from having migraines or diabetes or any preexisting medical issue. If you have a history with or are currently dealing with these, please exercise wisdom in deciding what the cause of your blurred vision or other symptoms may be. If this were easy, everybody would be doing it. There will be some physical struggle involved. Fighting through, continuing on, and persevering is more than worth it because He is the rewarder of those who diligently seek Him![67]

Healing

Another benefit of fasting is the healing process that it triggers. During a fast, energy is diverted away from the digestive system. Since there is no food to break down, the body uses energy for the metabolism and the immune system. This is one reason why animals stop eating when they are wounded and the reason we feel less hungry when we're sick.[68] Fasting is a powerful means that has been used to bring healing

---

[67] Heb. 11:6

[68] "Fasting For Detox," *Pure Inside Out,* http://www.pureinsideout.com/fasting-for-detox.html.

to the body. In some instances, fasting promotes accelerated healing and is a valuable treatment for a variety of medical conditions. Fasting works because the body has the capacity to heal when the obstacles to healing are removed.

During the first twenty-four to forty-eight hours of fasting, glycogen stores (the body's stored glucose for energy) are depleted. This sets off complex biochemical pathways in the body that aim to conserve energy while adequately fueling vital organs, and these conserving mechanisms may have beneficial side effects.[69] Many have experienced wonderful healing while fasting that has been documented by doctors and medical professionals.

There is so much that the body can have restored during a time of fasting. When the body has the ability to focus its energy on itself, you would be amazed at some of the things that can be regenerated and healed. Things cited most often for healing during fasting are: allergies, arthritis, digestive disorders of all kinds, skin conditions, cardiovascular disease, asthma, and much more. Because fasting initiates the body's own healing mechanisms, any ailment may show improvement.[70]

---

[69] "Taking the 'Fast Track' to Improved Immunity, *Dr. Fuhrman,* https://www.drfuhrman.com/library/fasting.aspx.

[70] "The Benefits of Fasting," *All About Fasting,* http://www.allaboutfasting.com/benefits-of-fasting.html.

In the fasting state, the body scours for dead cells, damaged tissues, fatty deposits, tumors and abscesses, all of which are burned for fuel or expelled as waste. Diseased cells are dissolved in a systematic manner, leaving healthy tissue.[71] During a fast a metamorphosis occurs. The body undergoes a tearing down and rebuilding of damaged materials. For this reason, fasting is known for giving the body a more youthful tone.

Energy

Fasting is a wonderful antidote for our usual over-indulgences. There is absolutely nothing wrong with the enjoyment of food, but when excess is experienced on a consistent basis, it does produce complications for the body. When the body has to regularly handle more than it is comfortable with or what is appropriate for it, it will suffer. When our bodies are overworked they tuck things away for another day. Whatever regular functional tasks can be postponed will be. It's like your body's own biological priority list. At mealtimes more work is dumped on them whether they are ready or not, which causes other tasks like healing to get pushed down the list. This is one of the

---

[71] "Healing Through Fasting," *FreedomYou*, http://www.freedomyou.com/healing_through_fasting_freedomyou.aspx.

reasons why fasting is so beautiful. Fasting is a gift for your weary, overworked body.

During fasting, we rest our system from the constant onslaught of food. Food is our primary source of energy, so it can be a new way of thinking to consider that the food we eat actually requires energy. Digesting, assimilating, and metabolizing—these activities require a great deal of energy. It is estimated that 65 percent of the body's energy must be directed to the digestive organs after a heavy meal.[72] Sixty-five percent is a pretty astonishing number to consider. It really taxes the body to have to digest and process the foods that we eat on a regular basis.

During a fast the body is able to distribute that digestive energy to other avenues. True, you will stop bringing in new energy sources, but all of the secondary functions will not compete with digestion in order to operate. So, at least for a period while your body has reserve fat and energy stores to draw from, the body will do many things that require less calories seemingly more efficiently than ever. This is why some people have reported feeling increases in energy levels while fasting. Crazy to think that you would gain energy when not being fueled by food, but that can temporarily be the case when the body has

---

[72] "The Benefits of Fasting," *All About Fasting,* http://www.allabout-fasting.com/benefits-of-fasting.html.

the ability to focus on itself rather than the constant process of digestion.

During and Closing

While fasting there are some simple keys to remember that can go a long way in helping us experience success. You will definitely want to make sure that you are staying hydrated. Drinking plenty of water throughout the day will aid your body in flushing toxins and dead cells. It will also help keep your immune system, nervous system, and other body functions performing while it adjusts to the fast.

It is important to minimize the intake of sugary beverages while fasting. Again, you are purging your system. The body is dependent on converting all food into sugar for fuel, and diets high in excess sugars usually come with strong emotional dependencies tied to sugar intake. This can be a tough fight for you if you have never given thought to the amount of sugar that you are consuming on a daily basis.

Just like entering and sustaining a fast requires wisdom, so does ending a fast, or concluding. If you have been fasting for a few days, you want to make sure that when you decide to break your fast and have a meal that you are very aware of what you introduce back into your system. This becomes especially important if you have been in any type of extended fast, let's say seven days or more. You do not want to shock your body and experience challenges that can be avoided with the right approach. You are never going to go wrong by taking it easy and slowly allowing yourself to get back into your normal eating rhythm. Again, your system has been operating at a different pace without certain foods, or food at all, for the duration of your fast. Getting back to normal may take anywhere from a few days to a week or more, and this is perfectly okay.

I know that you will be excited to break your fast, but do your body a favor and don't grab something greasy or fried. Fast food is probably not the best choice to eat as you're breaking a fast. Super dense, rich, and sugary food should be avoided for a few days as well. Don't succumb to the temptation to take several trips through the buffet line to celebrate. I promise it will not be a wise decision.

Just like entering and sustaining a fast requires wisdom, so does ending a fast, or concluding.

Of course, differing fasts can be safely broken in different ways. If you have been Daniel fasting, or sunup to sundown fasting, there are not going to be as many issues to avoid upon breaking your fast. If you have been absolute fasting or even liquid fasting for any extended period of time, your body is going to be less prepared to handle regular meals right away.

Smoothies are a great idea. Pureed soups without butter, meat, or cream are perfect. Steamed or lightly sautéed vegetables are great at this point. Fruits are really good, though be cautious with highly acidic choices. Wait a few days for breads, rice, pastas, etc. You can get back to them soon enough, just not the first day or two.

> **Do not resurrect anything that Jesus has laid to rest.**

Try to stay away from things that would clog your system and be harder to digest. Again, I am not claiming to provide you with all of the information that is out there regarding a fast. I want to present you with some simple, practical tools to make sure you know some of the best processes and practices that will help you to be successful in starting a lifestyle of fasting.

This may be completely brand new information for you, and maybe you've already been practicing these things for a while. Either way, I would encourage you to glean as much as you can from these tips, and also to apply yourself to prayer and the search for more helpful information. There are many great websites, books, and other resource materials available that can continue to equip and empower you to walk this way.

So What?

It is awesome to think that while the Lord might call you into what some view as an unbearable sacrifice, He has at the same time designed your body to reap incredible benefits in this process. In His amazing goodness He bids you to come; and then He heals, restores, and rejuvenates your body the entire time that you are answering His call. Praise God! What an amazing invitation indeed!

Another area in which fasting can often help us immensely is with our general lifestyle and eating habits. If there are any lifestyle changes you have been struggling to make, particularly with eating, fasting can be a great place to begin heading in that direction. After resetting your system and detoxing your body, what better time is there to abandon old methods, cravings, and lifestyle practices? Once you have conquered those desires and the holds they have, why willingly submit yourself to captivity again after concluding a time of fasting and prayer? I believe that fasting will help you to see the light at the end of the tunnel and that you will apprehend the freedom that has been made available to you by Jesus. What is conquered and dead is conquered and dead. Do not resurrect anything that Jesus has laid to rest.

Again, I am not encouraging you to respond to the Lord so that you can become the beneficiary of all of these benefits. I am simply submitting to you the wonderful truths of how God Himself has designed this experience of fasting and the benefits therein. I desire to encourage you to go after Him and lay hold of all that He has for you in greater ways than you have up to this point in your life. No matter how deep you may be in relationship with Christ, there is more!

10

Expectations

Expectation
1. Something expected; a thing looked forward to.
2. The degree of probability that something will occur.

Have you ever really wanted something to happen but instead ended up disappointed? Have you ever felt as if you put all of your hopes and desires in a certain direction or outcome, only to experience a serious letdown when things turned out differently? I think that you have. All of us have because we are human and disappointment is a staple of the human experience.

All disappointment stems from the failure of some expectation. Expectations are unavoidable. Every day, in fact, we are confronted with our expectations and how we will respond to them. Some expectations get fulfilled. Some expectations do not get met. Some are large and seem important, while others involve smaller, less urgent needs. Daily there is the experience of having to battle through the thought processes of building, breaking, and fulfilling expectations and the way that we have learned to manage those experiences.

Then, of course, some expectations are internally focused and others are external. At times we have all had thoughts about how someone would respond to a situation, only to find out that we were terribly wrong when it did not go as planned. We have all been in the place where we assumed a certain thing about somebody or something, only to be very surprised or let down when what we assumed turned out to not be true at all. What happens, then, is the decision to look past the disappointment or to carry a new opinion or offense based on unmet expectations. These are all examples of how expectations, or creating an expectation, can affect our lives.

Creating an expectation is not in and of itself a bad thing. Expectations can actually be a very good thing if they come from the right place and if they are handled correctly. How can expectation be handled negatively?

A negative situation arises when you create an unrealistic expectation and set it on a person, then expect that person to live up to your standards, not God's. Expectations can lead you to try to control outcomes because of how you desire or think a person should respond in any given scenario.

An unrealistic expectation can be very damaging to the individual who creates it. When an expectation goes unfulfilled it has the potential to leave us in a place of frustration, confusion, anger, and discouragement. There are many other feelings that can be experienced as a result of an unfulfilled expectation. These kinds of things threaten relationships and can warp our ability to compassionately view people and vulnerably approach God.

You will find that people do not always fit into your expectations of them. Rarely are you able to conform people or situations to your expectations. It takes time and surrender to mature to the point where we can have expectations go unfulfilled and not walk away with some sense of disappointment. In all of our expectations we have to learn to believe in the Lord, not a certain outcome or person that can let us down.

It would be an injustice for us to come this far in our journey without bridging the gap between expectations and fasting. Learning to have right expectations in fasting, and especially in the specific, practical ways that we are about to lay out, is something that I find missing from most of the talk on this subject. I have found that one of the hardest things for people to deal with in life is a failed expectation.

> **Remaining face-to-face with Jesus is the only hope that you have in seeing continued change in your life.**

As a believer, I have found that a failed expectation in your walk with God is something that many people struggle to recover from altogether. We must be sober-minded about what we are getting ourselves into and what the potential outcomes will be. We will not always accomplish every goal with every fast. Sometimes we may fall short. Fasting as a lifestyle should be approached as an opportunity to walk through something new with the Lord every time we fast.

As important as it is to hear from the Lord and obey Him through the process, we need to be ready to learn about our strengths and weaknesses, and to discover that ultimately it will only be the grace of God that leads us to growth in the lifestyle of fasting. Again, it is the truth that has the power to set us free, not our plan or willpower.

Fasting is not a once-in-a-lifetime sacrifice that is going to somehow, someway rid your life of all of the problems and things that you used to deal with before. There is a mind-set that we commonly adopt that tells us that nothing will ever be the same after we complete a fast. This is often true. We all enter a fast with some anticipation because we realize the significance of what lies ahead.

I know how important it is to build excitement and momentum as you enter into a fast. However, I think that is a good thing to recognize a few things about life after a fast so that you do not end up disappointed and frustrated with God after you conclude. Fasting is a lot more than the actual time you go without eating. We have spoken about the approach. The landing and return to life is just as important. I want to be transparent in looking at the whole process because coming to any point of the fasting experience with unbalanced expectations can set a person up for the disappointment we mentioned before.

Back to Normal

One of the things that I find shocks people the most after coming out of a fast is that they become normal again. During a time of fasting there is the real potential to feel like a spiritual superman. There can be an intense spiritual awareness to the closeness of Jesus, a strong desire to keep yourself in the place of worship, prayer, reading of the Scriptures, and living uncharacteristically spiritual and disciplined. However, once the fast has ended, at some point you are going to have to return to being a normal person. I find that many people do not know how to handle this challenge.

When I say that you are going to feel normal again, what I mean is that you are going to enter back into a regular rhythm of life and the challenges that are found there. It is at this point that we need to be very aware of what is actually happening so that we are not deceived.

When I concluded my first extended fast I had a hard time adjusting back into what I considered normal. Again, it is not that the proximity of Jesus changed because I was now eating again. It is just the awareness and perspective that I had to meet with Him. I found the high that I walked on during the time of fasting came back down to earth after I concluded. But once the fast is finished, it is time to walk with Jesus in everyday life and steward those things that have been done both in you and through you in your time of fasting.

When you do not feel like praying or reading your Bible you will want to ask yourself, "Why is this happening?" When you simply just cannot seem to find the focus to be with Jesus, you will turn your frustration inward and want to know, "Why isn't there something different about me?" We must be very careful during this period of time that we do not allow the enemy to manipulate our thoughts and emotions. The enemy will want you to believe that nothing happened during your time of fasting. The enemy, and the lies that he will come at you with, are aiming for you to actually come into agreement that you have not changed at all. In fact, the enemy will insist feeling normal again is just clear evidence that it was all fanaticism in the first place. You have to be very aware and diligent to guard your heart in these moments.

Do not allow a current victory to stunt your growth.

It is absolutely true that God is working in you during times of fasting to produce within you the image of His Son. You are being molded by the hands of an amazing father during your times of fasting and it is undeniable that these times will greatly change you. More than you can even comprehend is happening during your time of fasting. There are layers of things simultaneously happening in and around you while fasting. This is why it is important to keep at it and to incorporate fasting as a lifestyle as a follower of Jesus.

We have been called into a lifestyle of fasting. Fasting is not a one-time sacrificial offering that is expected to change your life forever. Remaining face-to-face with Jesus is the only hope that you have in seeing continued change in your life. Obedience to His commands keeps you face-to-face with Him.

No More Need

We all battle the tendency to settle into a place of rest in current accomplishments. You do not want to allow the enemy to keep you camped out in a place of victory to the point where you lose sight of the need to continue fighting forward. Again, fasting as a lifestyle means exactly that; that we are giving the rest of our life to the continued experience of Jesus in the place and practice of fasting. I am not saying that we are fasting forever. There are seasons for fasting, and fasting more intensely, as well as seasons without. But "lifestyle" fasting means weaving fasting into the fabric of our lives as a consistent discipline, just like prayer.

As we do this, it can become easier to complete a fast and be satisfied with your accomplishment. If we aren't careful this can desensitize us to ignore the invitation to fast again anytime soon. Spiritually I see this happen all the time. People complete what they consider to be a mountaintop experience, a lifetime achievement, and then they settle in and become complacent. They lose hunger.

There is something about a victory in your life that you need to be very careful about. Please take note here. Do not allow a current victory to stunt your growth.

We have all seen someone do this in different parts of life. Sure, you may not relate to the exact example I am talking about, but you have nonetheless seen it. A sports team wins the championship one year, and then for the next several years in a row they cannot seem to get it together and make the playoffs or even produce a winning record. What is it that happens in this situation? How do you involve the same people and yet come to such a radically different conclusion?

We must be aware and in tune with the leading of the Spirit so that we do not lose our hunger. The Holy Spirit will always invite us into places to draw us closer to Jesus. One of the primary roles of the work of the Holy Spirit in our lives is to daily reveal Jesus to us. This place of revealing will most often come through the daily invitations to obey in different areas of your life.

There is nothing wrong with becoming satisfied with the person of Jesus, and actually I would greatly encourage you to do so. But there is a great danger in allowing a satisfaction with your own accomplishments during your walk with Jesus to sap your passion for anything above your current experience. Being satisfied with Jesus and becoming satisfied with yourself, or your victories, are two very

> **The Holy Spirit will always invite us into places to draw us closer to Jesus.**

different things. The former leads to liberty while the latter leads back to bondage. Never allow what you have done to keep you from moving forward. Do not rest in your victories and become stagnant. **Do not allow victory to bring complacency into your life.** Do not think that because you have obeyed in one moment that it somehow exempts you from future moments of obedience.

It is easy to feel like you have filled a quota when you complete a fast. Fasting is not a checkpoint item on a to-do list. You can't just think that you do not have to worry about fasting again because you've accomplished a one-time goal. When we view fasting as a lifestyle, we will joyfully walk with Jesus in the place of His invitation to us even when we feel as if we have conquered mountains.

Some even think that fasting is only for January. It is popular in current church culture to embrace the place of fasting in the month of January as a "first fruits" offering to the Lord. I would heartily "amen" this effort. My question for you is not so much what your January looks like. My question for you is, what does your February through December look like? It's kind of like the mentality that Sunday is set apart for church while Monday through Saturday are a little less spiritual. However, the fasting you do in January does not exempt you from walking with Jesus the rest of the calendar year. You may not like the direction this is heading. If not, I am not going to offer you an apology. I am attempting to speak the truth in love to you so that we all may be able to grow up into Him who is the head, Jesus Christ.[73]

The Real Deal

Any single fast has the potential to completely change a person. When we are walking with Jesus we have to allow Him to be the one to mold us and do the forming in our life. This mind-set will prevent you from experiencing a colossal crash in your life. Having this in mind will keep you from being upset about God not doing something that you may really want in any given moment. Jesus is the one who is leading and in charge.

Applying your life to the repeated process of fasting will guarantee powerful results. You cannot just throw your life into fasting as a lifestyle and remain the same. There is no way that you will continue to meet with Jesus in the place of fasting and not see tangible

---

[73] Eph. 4:15

breakthroughs and results. This will affect the very substance of your person.

Although this is how we posture our hearts as we enter into fasting, let us always be mindful that stewardship is key. You must continue to cultivate all that God is working in you. It will take a diligent effort on your part to flesh out all of the things you know God has worked into you during times of fasting.

The end goal of fasting is to meet with Jesus and be conformed to the image of His person.

I would like to repeat: You must walk out all that God has worked in. Fasting will not exempt you from daily walking with Jesus once you have crossed the finish line. Fasting does not release you from the responsibility of abiding. Fasting is a means to an end. The end goal of fasting is to meet with Jesus and be conformed to the image of His person. Anything less than this is simply not worth our efforts. If there were not the promise of being able to meet with the living Christ and to know Him in the fellowship of his sufferings,[74] this would all be without purpose.

I want to reiterate that the means is not the end. You are not just fasting to say that you have fasted.

---

[74] Phil. 3:10

Expectations

Developing your spiritual résumé in the eyes and minds of others is not the goal. You are not fasting to impress someone. You are not fasting because the pressure of the crowd around you is telling you to fast. You are fasting as a means to an end, and the end of your fasting leads to Christ. Meet Him there; He is waiting for you.

11

Purifying

Remember, we established that fasting is much more than a simple *turning from food*. Fasting may be a *turning from*, but it is equally as much, and I would say more importantly, a *turning to the Lord*. When fasting, we are not just turning from food; we are turning to Jesus! This is incredibly important and something that is worth mentioning again. In fasting, we have been given a divine medium by which Jesus purifies His bride and makes us ready for Himself as a people that He will return for. We are the people of God, the bride of Christ. In our positioning in the earth as the bride, it is imperative that we understand the implications of a right posture.

I would like to return to a verse that we touched on briefly earlier in our journey together. In Matthew chapter 9 we find Jesus being confronted by John's disciples about their lack of fasting. Jesus' response is fascinating to me and something that we will unpack a little further.

Jesus turns to those who are attempting to criticize Him and His disciples for their lack of fasting activity as He says these words, "The attendants of the bridegroom cannot mourn as long as the bridegroom is with them, can they? But the days will come when the bridegroom is taken away from them, and then they will fast."[75] Jesus is telling them that there is no reason for them to fast because He is with them. However, He says there is coming a day when He will leave their side, and then undoubtedly they will fast. Why is this? What would be the reason that Jesus could use in order to validate His point for the need to fast once He was gone? I believe the answer returns us to our posture as the bride in preparation.

When Jesus was with the disciples they experienced a certain level of closeness. He walked next to them. They were able to tangibly look into one another's face as they spoke. There were moments in conversation they may have joined hands, leaned in, and focused intently. It only makes sense that the disciples experienced something that none of us really

---

[75] Matt. 9:15

have available to us. Jesus was an incarnate God in the flesh; the person of Jesus living beside them for three years.

The truth that Jesus is pointing out to us in His response above is something that we must not just read over. Jesus says that when He goes His followers will fast. Herein lies the beauty. Herein lies the hidden treasure. Herein lies the reality for us today. Jesus is the bridegroom, and we are the bride. This is intimate talk. This is bridal language. Jesus was illustrating His point with this language to give us a glimpse of the experiential pleasures of His person to be found in the place of fasting.

> **Fasting is the means by which Jesus has made it available for us to draw near.**

Jesus knew that the disciples had a special experience of His person while He was with them. The disciples experienced the presence of Jesus in a way that is unparalleled. Jesus also knew that there would be a loss when He was removed, and so He provided them, and all of us, with the answer on how to close the gap, if you would. His response to John's disciples shows that He actually hid the answer to the puzzling question right out in the open.

Fasting is the means by which Jesus has made it available for us to draw near. Fasting is what shortens the distance in our experience of His person and His presence. Fasting is what allows for our level of intimacy with Him to be heightened. Fasting is what locks our eyes with His! In fasting, we find the positioning of the bride for the return of the Bridegroom. Fasting is a posture that cries out for the return of the lover of our souls!

Encounter with the Bridegroom

I would like to share an experience that I had recently on the thirty-seventh day of a forty-day liquid fast. My family and I attended a local church gathering in our area that Sunday morning. During the musical portion of the worship service there was a rich presence of Jesus that filled the room as the worship team began to lead the saints in song with them. It was one of those mornings where I felt I could've lingered in that place for the rest of my life.

At one point during this time of worship, I stood absolutely still and closed my eyes to set my attention completely on Jesus. As I did this I was brought into a vision. Like Paul says in 2 Corinthians, "Whether it was in the body or out of the body I do not know—God knows."[76] The only thing that is important to me is that I know it happened.

---

[76] 2 Cor. 12:2, NIV

As I came into the vision I was walking on an old rugged pathway. I was weary, yet determined. The road was narrow. I knew this road I was traveling had to do with the fast that I was soon to finish. As I lifted my head I could see in the distance what looked like a break in the pathway; an opening with a bright light. When I drew nearer to the opening my heart began to burn with an intense excitement. I knew that I had been traveling for quite some time. I knew that out in front of me was some sort of finish line. I could see the conclusion to the journey that I had been on.

Closing in on the opening I saw what looked like a person standing off to the side. The person seemed to be positioned almost as if to be waiting for someone. With the end in sight I put my head down and took a few steps that brought me to the opening at the end of the road. Just as I made it to the end of the pathway I turned to see who it was that was standing there. When I lifted my head I found myself standing face-to-face with Jesus.

> **Fasting is a posture that cries out for the return of the lover of our souls!**

There was an overwhelming sense of joy. His face was radiant. He didn't say a word, and He didn't have to. I had a knowledge in the moment of all that His heart was communicating. The smile on His face seemed to tell me everything I needed to know. It was as if I could hear His heart communicating these thoughts to me, "Well done, Mike. You made it. Well done, Mike. You were faithful." I felt Him telling me, "Well done, Mike. You walked this rugged road and have now come to the end." There was a warm sense of celebration. I knew that Jesus was there to welcome me. This was a moment where all of the struggles from the journey were finished and I had my reward.

The captivation of His face was immense. I felt complete. There was a drawing to Him that was magnetic. As we stood in the middle of the pathway He lifted His right hand as if to grant me passage. I looked and saw what was a flourishing green pasture as far as the eye could see. There was a great calm; a rest that is hard to communicate. I looked back at Jesus. I then looked to my right at the rugged pathway that I had just completed. I was quickly reminded of the journey, the suffering I had endured, and the countless opportunities along the way to abandon the path.

I looked back into the face of Jesus. I stood in the middle of the road, looking back and forth over the green pasture and the rugged pathway. I couldn't make up my mind as to which direction I really wanted to go. As I brought myself to the point of decision my eyes began to fill with tears. I looked up into the face of Jesus and tried to come up with something to say.

All of my desire for eloquence seemed to escape me in that moment. I was gripped with such a deep sense of longing. I stood in the middle of the opening with a decision to make as to what direction I would go. The only words that I could muster up in the moment were, "Lord, I don't want to continue on without You…don't let me go either way without You. Please don't leave me by myself."

The well of tears that my eyes were holding back had now released down my face. I broke down weeping before the Lord as I shared the vulnerability of my heart with Him. As I began to cry harder I bent over and put my face into my hands. As I did this I could again hear the sound of worship happening all around me. I lifted my face from my hands to find that I was now back in the local church gathering. This is a moment that I will remember for the rest of my life. This is a moment that has forever marked my heart.

Dialed In

Fasting absolutely has the power to sift things that do not really matter and remove them from my focus. Fasting is one of the powerful ways the Lord continually sets my sights upon those things that matter most—namely His presence and His voice. When those two things are central, everything else in life falls into its rightly aligned place.

Notice I did not say His presence and voice must be first. Jesus does not fit into a priority list. In fact, He transcends the entire list. There would be no list without Him. Jesus is central in life and purpose; He is everything. As He is everything to us and for us, every lesser concern must find its place and purpose flowing out of His centrality in our lives. Regardless of your role in life, it must find its expression through the centrality of Christ. The centrality of Christ is made real to us in the place of surrender or yielding to Him in every area of our heart and life.

Jesus is central in life and purpose; He is everything.

Christ becoming central in our lives is no small statement. In order for Christ to become central it means that there has been a shift from what used to sit in the center of my life. It means "I" must be dethroned and replaced. Christ becoming central means that an eviction has been given to the self-absorbed reality that I am currently living in. Self-centeredness can be conquered by and through fasting.

The "me" sitting in the center of my life and all of life's details revolving around me is not something that people easily let go of. Don't think that just because you have adopted the right Jesus-follower language that you have conquered the love of self. Don't think that because you have a great attendance at your Sunday services that you have conquered the love of self.

Giving regularly or giving more when you feel led does not necessarily mean that you have conquered the love of self. The reality is that you can have all of these things in place and still love yourself more than you love Jesus. I know that might seem a little extreme. But if you've spent any time in front of the cross, or even a mirror, I bet you know what I mean. But there will always be excuses that rise to the surface, trying to keep "self" in the driver's seat.

Special Company

Many look at the Lord's invitation to fast and make the determination that it is only for a select group such as pastors, preachers, or those with the right circumstances in life. This is one of the greatest ways that we deceive ourselves and create exemptions to excuse us from greater things. I want to let you in on a little secret: There is no special group. The invitation is freely given to all. Regardless of what it is in life that you have been called to do, the first and greatest call of life is to come to Jesus. We are all called to be loved by Him, and to love Him in return. Being a Jesus lover takes priority over whatever it is that He may have asked you to do for Him. Loving Jesus is the highest call of life.

At the end of the book of Luke we find these words, "No one, after putting his hand to the plow and looking back, is fit for the kingdom of God."[77] It is undeniable that when coming into the Kingdom of God we are going to find our hands at the plow; there will certainly be something for us to do. However, man has always seemed to get hung up idolizing the plow. This is one of the reasons why we exempt ourselves from certain invitations from the Lord. It's not the job that God assigns that is special. Each of us is His child and each of us has a "plow" He designed.

Loving Jesus is the highest call of life.

It does not matter if you are a preacher, if you are a pastor, if you work a sandwich line at a fast-food restaurant, if you sit in a cubicle all day, or if you run a multi-billion-dollar organization; the call of coming to the Lord, and becoming one with Him is issued to all of His sons and daughters.

We may be able to weasel ourselves out of other conversations based off of particulars that are specific to certain callings and activities, but we cannot exempt ourselves from the talk of intimacy with Jesus. Intimacy with Jesus is offered to all of His followers. Experiential union with Christ is something that

---

[77] Luke 9:62

we have, without a doubt, all been invited into. The pathway of fasting is one way that Jesus offers to all of us in order to experience more of this union.

The truth is, many just love themselves too much to fast. Many have a lot of "right" activity and impressive language, yet at the core of who they are they love themselves more than they love experiencing Jesus. There is a love of self that wants to benefit from Jesus, just not lay it all down for Him. There is a love of self that wants Jesus to receive the crown of thorns, the nails, and the cross for me. However, simultaneously this self-love isn't willing to push away the plate for Him. Laying it all down for Jesus involves cultivating an unconditional yes in my heart to anything that draws us together.

An unconditional yes means nothing held back. Jesus is looking for a man or woman that won't try to set the terms of how they want to follow Him. Jesus is searching the earth for a person who isn't always trying to negotiate the easiest pathway. Many who follow are there because there is some perceived benefit that they are waiting to acquire that they think will come if they do things for Him. But we need to be saying yes to Jesus Himself.

We cannot exempt ourselves from the talk of intimacy with Jesus.

Being a lover of benefits and blessings does not necessarily mean that you love Jesus. It just means that you love the things that Jesus offers and does for you. Always remember, there were plenty of people that followed Jesus everywhere He went. Plenty of people remained with Him, but were never considered disciples.

Greater than the opinion of our culture is the opinion of Jesus.

They were always waiting for Him to do something so that they could benefit. We must diligently search our hearts in these matters. We have to be ruthless and honest with ourselves about our current condition. It is the truth that has the power to set us free—not thinking more highly of yourself than you ought because of things Jesus has done for you.

Our culture has defined what a Jesus-follower should look like, act like, and sound like. As long as you attend a certain way, as long as you give a certain way, and as long as you don't offend people a certain way, you can be mistaken for a Christian. Greater than the opinion of our culture is the opinion of Jesus. And if it is Jesus that we are following and desiring to please with our lives, then we should allow Him to provide us with an accurate definition of what being one of His followers is really all about.

"Wow, weren't we talking about fasting?" Yes, we absolutely are talking about fasting. And what I have found is that there is a love of self that sits upon the throne of men's hearts that grants them the right to feel they can deny the invitation of the Lord to meet Him in the place of fasting. Again, simply put, people love themselves too much to fast. The attitudes and the excuses we use to avoid fasting are connected.

Self-Made

When we really boil it all down, Jesus knows that fasting will make you what you could never make yourself. Fasting is one of the ways we embrace the cross and die to ourselves. If you do not see any benefit in dying to yourself, then I encourage you to stay away from fasting. A death to self awaits you there. It is unavoidable, and it will not be hidden. By the sweet embrace of the cross you will find that the strength of the grip with which you once held onto all of your own ways will be released. This is God's way. This is a direction that God leads those who want to become more like His Son, Jesus.

The lie of the enemy has been the same since the beginning of time. You can make yourself. You don't need God. You can be your own god. You can lead yourself, govern yourself, and make your own way. Listen closely to these words: "You can make yourself." At the root of it, that is what most of us believe. We believe that if you give us enough time and practice. If we just apply ourselves and modify to the right behaviors. If we can just get around the right people long enough or settle into the right geographical location. The list is endless.

However, consider these same words in a slightly different context. In the book of Isaiah, we find someone saying something that is very similar. Isaiah chapter 14 shows us an individual who felt as if they could make themselves something great. Isaiah gives us a glimpse of the prideful human condition, which began with Lucifer, "I will ascend above the tops of the clouds; I will make myself like the Most High."[78] "I will make myself" has been the intention of the devil for mankind from the beginning. It was his own ambition and is why he was cast down out of the heavens. The devil wanted to exalt himself above God and felt as if he could make himself like the Most High. The desire to be self-made was originated by the devil. He desires to drag us all into this same trap.

We are not to be self-made. In utter dependency, we are to throw our lives upon and into the person of Jesus. Just as the hands of God formed us and knit us together while we were in our mother's womb, God is

---

[78] Isa. 14:14

desiring to carry, nurture, and shape us. We are to continually place our trust in Him to form us and knit us into the image of Jesus as we walk in obedience to His voice daily. God can and will continually make the man who relinquishes his own ability and control to be like Jesus.

> **There is a forming in fasting that comes by the hands of the Lord that all of your life's efforts will never be able to match.**

There is a forming in fasting that comes by the hands of the Lord that all of your life's efforts will never be able to match. You may very well have enough willpower and resolve to become an impressive spiritual person to those around you. Being impressive to those around you will never be synonymous with becoming everything that God can make you. I encourage you not to simply find a place of rest and satisfaction in the opinion of the crowd; keep pressing on with Him and into Him.

Don't settle for being a self-made version of God's child. Don't ignore the prompting and the leading of the Lord to meet Him in the place of fasting. He is inviting you because He loves you and wants to encounter you. He is welcoming you to the pathway of fasting because He knows there is more that He desires for you to become. Become one with Him and then become something for Him. He is waiting for you out in the deep waters! Feast upon Him who is the bread that comes down from heaven!

My dear friend, it is time to fast and pray!

About the Author

Michael is the Founding Director of Burning Ones. At the age of twenty-one Michael was a drug addict, dealer, diseased, and hopeless. It was at this time that he had an encounter with Jesus that radically changed his life. From this point forward he has been relentless in his pursuit of the God-Man, Jesus Christ. Michael now preaches Jesus around the world powerfully with great demonstrations of signs and miracles.

You can find out more about Burning Ones by visiting:

www.burningones.org
www.facebook.com/burningonesinternational

More about Michael:

www.facebook.com/michaelsdow
www.twitter.com/michaeldow
www.instagram.com/michaeldow

About the Ministry

Burning Ones is the ministry of Michael and Anna Dow. Our vision is to raise up burning ones that will make Jesus famous among the nations of the world. We do that by preaching the Gospel of the Kingdom until the hearts of men and women come alive to God and burn with passion for His Son, Jesus, by the power of the Holy Spirit. We preach Jesus in church services, conferences, and mass crusades around the world with extraordinary signs and miracles.

When He consumes our lives, we become His burning ones! We are burning ones by experience and expression. We experience Him and then we express Him to the world. Burning Ones is not something that is exclusive for us to a specific time and space; it is life itself!

Website: www.burningones.org
Facebook: burningonesinternational
E-mail: info@burningones.org

FREE INDEED

Does God have to have your agreement in order for Him to have your obedience? Will you obey the call of God even if there is not an instant payout or benefit to you? Many are willing to step into obedience and do what God is asking so long as they are the primary beneficiaries of their obedience. Are you willing to walk with a God that you cannot control? Can you handle walking with a Jesus that you cannot manipulate and leverage your faithfulness against? There is a confrontation that awaits you in the text...a confrontation to determine what kind of Jesus follower you are going to be. In the book *Free Indeed*, Michael challenges the reader to surrender everything to Jesus and invest the rest of their life into uncompromised obedience to Him.

Available at:

Amazon
Kindle
iBooks
www.burningones.org

THE BREAKING POINT

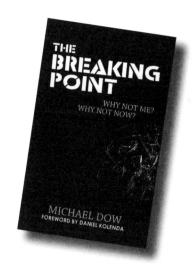

Every generation God seeks after a man or a woman that He can use to partner with Him in changing the world. Our lives are the point through which God is desperately longing to break into a generation! What would it look like if God were to truly break into the heart of a man? How would that man impact a generation? Michael challenges the reader to believe that they are the breaking point, right here, right now!

Available at:

Amazon

Kindle

iBooks

www.burningones.org